D0079791

Financial Accounting

NINTH EDITION

OR

Accounting: Concepts and Applications

NINTH EDITION

W. Steve Albrecht

Brigham Young University

James D. Stice

Brigham Young University

Earl K. Stice

Brigham Young University

Monte Swain

Brigham Young University

THOMSON

SOUTH-WESTERN

Australia · Canada · Mexico · Singapore · Spain · United Kingdom · United States

THOMSON

SOUTH-WESTERN

Study Guide for **Financial Accounting, 9e** or **Accounting: Concepts and Applications, 9e**

W. Steve Albrecht, James D. Stice, Earl K. Stice, and Monte R. Swain

VP/Editorial Director:
Jack W. Calhoun

VP/Editor-in-Chief:
George Werthman

Executive Editor:
Sharon Oblinger

Developmental Editor:
Carol Bennett

Technology Project Editor:
Amy Wilson

Marketing Manager:
Keith Chasse

Senior Production Editor:
Kara ZumBahlen

Media Editor:
Kelly Reid

Compositor:
Marci Combs

Manufacturing Coordinator:
Doug Wilke

Printer:
Globus Printing, Minster, OH

For permission to use material from this text or product, submit a request online at http://www.thomsonrights.com.

For more information
contact South-Western,
5191 Natorp Boulevard,
Mason, Ohio 45040.
Or you can visit our Internet site at:
http://www.swlearning.com

CONTENTS

To the Student

The study of accounting involves four major elements:

1. Understanding the role of accounting in business.
2. Learning the terms associated with accounting.
3. Understanding the concepts, procedures, and financial statements that are used to record and summarize economic events.
4. Being able, on the basis of that understanding, to record and summarize economic transactions in accordance with generally accepted accounting principles.

Accounting is considered by most students to be a challenging course, partly because there is a lot to learn, and partly because accounting knowledge is cumulative—that is, concepts and procedures in later chapters are built upon what has been learned in earlier chapters. This makes it impractical to cram for an accounting exam; you must learn as you go, each day building on what you learned yesterday and last week and last month.

The challenge, therefore, is to keep up with the work, not to fall behind in doing the assigned reading and the problems, even though this course will probably require more of your time than most others. This Study Guide should help you to understand the material and to retain what you have learned by providing opportunities to review the subject matter in several different ways. Through it, you will be able to test your understanding of the concepts and your ability to perform the corresponding procedures.

The authors of the textbook are also the authors of this Study Guide; we wrote it to facilitate and reinforce your understanding of the text in every way possible. While we initially had in mind those students who have difficulty with the course, we have found the guide also useful to those who learn accounting fairly readily.

Each Study Guide chapter should be reviewed after you have read the corresponding text chapter. We recommend that you use the Study Guide chapters in the following way:

1. Read the *learning objectives* to pinpoint the areas where study is needed. For most chapters, the learning objectives are identified as Basic or Expanded to correspond with the Basic and Expanded material of the text.
2. Read the concise, point-by-point *chapter review* carefully. It will help you decide which areas you understand well and which require more study. These reviews also will be useful when preparing for exams.
3. If you are having problems with certain topics, read *common errors* for suggestions on ways to better understand the material.

4. Work through each of the four sets of questions to test your knowledge.

   a. *Match* the key terms with their definitions in order to test your mastery of the new words intro-
      duced in the chapter. Your understanding of, and ability to use, accounting terms is important to
      your success in this course. Accounting is the language of business, and if you don't understand
      the language, you'll find it difficult to understand the concepts and problems.
   b. Answer the *true-false* questions.
   c. Answer the *multiple-choice* questions. If your answer to a question is "none of the above," think
      about what the correct answer should be.
   d. Complete each of the short *exercises*. These cover the major topics in the chapter and are similar
      to the exercises in the textbook. Each exercise should not take more than 15 to 20 minutes to
      complete.
   e. Finally, check your answers against those that appear at the end of each Study Guide chapter.

By using the Study Guide conscientiously, you will be reviewing what you have learned in each text
chapter in several different ways: with the point-by-point review, the matching definitions, the true-false
questions, the multiple-choice questions, and the short exercises. At first, it may take you three to four
hours to work through a chapter of the Study Guide. After you have finished four or five chapters, however, it will become apparent which sections are most helpful to you. You should then be able to complete
the Study Guide chapters more quickly. You may also find that some topics will come easier to you than
others. For those that are more difficult, extra time with the Study Guide may be needed.

The experiences of students who have used the Study Guide indicate that its regular use will improve your understanding of accounting and help you to achieve the best possible results in this course.

Good luck!

W. Steve Albrecht
James D. Stice
Earl K. Stice
Monte R. Swain

Chapter 1
Accounting Information: Users and Uses

LEARNING OBJECTIVES

After studying this chapter, you should be able to:

1. Describe the purpose of accounting and explain its role in business and society.

2. Identify the primary users of accounting information.

3. Describe the environment of accounting, including the effects of generally accepted accounting principles, international business, ethical considerations, and technology.

4. Analyze the reasons for studying accounting.

CHAPTER REVIEW

What's the Purpose of Accounting?

1. Accounting is a system for providing quantitative, financial information about economic entities that is useful for making sound business decisions. Accounting is often called the "language of business" because it provides the means of recording and communicating business activities and the results of those activities.

The Relationship of Accounting to Business

2. Organizations acquire and exchange resources. Accounting is used to keep track of an entity's resources and to see how well it is accomplishing its objectives.

Who Uses Accounting Information?

3. The outputs of the accounting process are financial reports, including the general-purpose financial statements, income tax returns, special reports provided to various regulatory agencies such as the Securities and Exchange Commission, and managerial reports.

4. Financial accounting focuses on the information needs of external financial statement users. Lenders (creditors) and investors are the primary external users of accounting information.

5. Management accounting focuses on the accounting information used by management in making decisions.

6. Other users of accounting information include suppliers and customers, employees, competitors, government agencies, and the press.

What Kind of Environment Does Accounting Operate Within?

7. Accounting is a dynamic, service-oriented discipline continuously evolving to meet the needs of those it serves.

The Significance and Development of Accounting Standards

8. Generally accepted accounting principles (GAAP) are guidelines to accounting practices that have been accepted by the accounting profession through time-tested applications. Accounting reports that are based on consistently applied GAAP provide investors and creditors with more comparable data.

9. Accounting principles have evolved over time. In recent years they have been influenced largely by such organizations as the FASB, SEC, AICPA, IMA, and IRS.

International Business

10. Business activity is expanding rapidly on a worldwide basis. The environment of accounting is based on a global economy.

11. Accounting practices often must be modified to reflect international operations and transactions. Attempts are being made to establish comparable accounting practices worldwide through the International Accounting Standards Committee (IASC).

Ethics in Accounting

12. There is a growing concern about ethics in our society. This concern is especially relevant for CPAs and CMAs because of the public trust professional accountants have been given.

13. CPAs and CMAs have adopted standards of conduct to guide their actions and help them fulfill their responsibilities to the public, to their clients, and to their colleagues in the accounting profession.

Technology

14. Advances in technology are impacting business and accounting in significant ways. Technology allows companies to gather vast amounts of information and to process it quickly and accurately. Technology also allows user access to data in new and exciting ways. However, technology has not replaced the need for judgment and accounting expertise.

So, Why Should I Study Accounting?

15. Everyone is affected to some degree by accounting information. Those who recognize the value of accounting information and learn how to use it to make better decisions will have a competitive advantage over those who do not.

COMMON ERRORS

This first chapter does not contain problem material. Its purpose is to provide an overview and perspective of accounting. The major difficulty in this chapter is unfamiliar accounting or business terminology. This is a basic challenge of the first several chapters, since you are beginning to learn about accounting, the language of business. Throughout the text, new terms are defined in the margins and highlighted at the end of each chapter to assist you in learning this new language.

SELF-TEST

Matching

Instructions: Write the letter of each of the following terms in the space to the left of its appropriate definition.

a. accounting
b. business
c. generally accepted accounting principles
d. management accounting
e. Financial Accounting Standards Board

f. accounting cycle
g. Securities and Exchange Commission
h. nonprofit organization
i. financial accounting

_____ 1. The private organization responsible for establishing the standards for financial accounting and reporting in the United States.

_____ 2. The area of accounting concerned with reporting financial information to interested external parties.

_____ 3. The government body responsible for regulating the financial reporting practices of most publicly-owned corporations in connection with the buying and selling of stocks and bonds.

_____ 4. An organization operated with the objective of making a profit from the sale of goods or services.

_____ 5. A system for providing quantitative, financial information about economic entities for decision-making purposes.

_____ 6. The area of accounting concerned with providing internal financial reports to assist management in making decisions.

_____ 7. The sequence of events in which accounting data are analyzed, recorded, classified, summarized, and reported.

_____ 8. Authoritative guidelines that define accounting practice at a particular time.

_____ 9. An entity without a profit objective, oriented toward providing services efficiently and effectively.

True/False

Instructions: Place a check mark in the appropriate column to indicate whether each of the following statements is true or false.

		True	False
1.	In a nonprofit organization, the primary goal is to earn income.	_____	_____
2.	All organizations need accounting to keep track of their resources and activities and to measure how well they are accomplishing their objectives.	_____	_____
3.	Accounting helps organizations determine how to best use their resources.	_____	_____
4.	Accounting provides all information, financial and otherwise, needed for decision making.	_____	_____
5.	The primary external user of accounting information is management.	_____	_____
6.	The income statement, the balance sheet, and the corporate tax return are the three general-purpose financial statements.	_____	_____
7.	Monetary resources are obtained through investments by owners, loans from creditors, and business earnings.	_____	_____
8.	General-purpose financial statements are prepared primarily to meet the needs of investors and creditors.	_____	_____
9.	Management accounting is the area of accounting concerned with reporting financial information to interested external parties.	_____	_____
10.	Today's business environment is more national than international.	_____	_____
11.	Generally accepted accounting principles (GAAP) are prescribed by law.	_____	_____
12.	The IRS is currently the primary standard-setting body for accounting principles in the private sector.	_____	_____
13.	The *Code of Professional Conduct* is to be followed by certified public accountants (CPAs).	_____	_____

Multiple Choice

Instructions: Circle the letter that best completes each of the following statements.

1. An example of a nonprofit organization is a

    a. grocery store.
    b. car dealership.
    c. hospital.
    d. machine shop.

2. Which of the following best describes accounting?

    a. A system for providing quantitative, financial information about entities for decision-making purposes
    b. A science used by management for determining future costs
    c. A form of mathematical economics
    d. A system of predicting future outcomes

3. The basic purpose of financial accounting is to

    a. provide financial information for use by decision makers.
    b. determine the amount of taxes to be paid.
    c. evaluate the worth of a company.
    d. determine the cash receipts and disbursements of corporations.

4. Which of the following groups is *not* considered an external user of accounting information?

    a. Creditors
    b. Investors
    c. Bankers
    d. Managers

5. Which of the following statements does *not* reflect the impact of technology on business and accounting?

    a. Technology allows organizations to gather vast amounts of transaction data.
    b. Technology allows for the processing of information in a quick and accurate manner.
    c. Technology eliminates the need for accountants.
    d. Technology is continuing to develop, which suggests future changes in the way business is conducted.

6. The accounting cycle provides all of the following outputs except

    a. budgets.
    b. the income statement.
    c. the statement of cash flows.
    d. Each of the above is provided.

7. Which of the following organizations is the most directly involved in developing worldwide accounting standards?

    a. FASB
    b. IASB
    c. SEC
    d. AICPA

8. Currently, the primary standard-setting body for accounting principles in the private sector is the

    a. SEC.
    b. AICPA.
    c. FASB.
    d. IRS.

9. Why is there growing concern over ethics as an environmental factor affecting accounting?

   a. Ethical considerations affect all society, including accounting and business.
   b. Ethical problems result from too much focus on short-term results.
   c. Major incidents of improper acts are highlighted by reporting in the news media.
   d. All of the above cause a growing concern over ethics.

Exercises

Because of the conceptual nature of this chapter, there are no workout exercises.

ANSWERS

Matching

1.	e	4.	b	7.	f
2.	i	5.	a	8.	c
3.	g	6.	d	9.	h

True/False

1.	F	6.	F	11.	F
2.	T	7.	T	12.	F
3.	T	8.	T	13.	T
4.	F	9.	F		
5.	F	10.	F		

Multiple Choice

1.	c	4.	d	7.	b
2.	a	5.	c	8.	c
3.	a	6.	a	9.	d

Chapter 2
Financial Statements: An Overview

LEARNING OBJECTIVES

After studying this chapter, you should be able to:

1. Understand the basic elements, uses, and limitations of the balance sheet.

2. Understand the basic elements and uses of the income statement.

3. Understand the categories and uses of the statement of cash flows and see how the primary financial statements tie together.

4. Recognize the need for financial statement notes and identify the types of information included in the notes.

5. Describe the purpose of an audit report and the incentives the auditors has to perform a good audit.

6. Explain the fundamental concepts and assumptions that underlie financial accounting.

CHAPTER REVIEW

The Financial Statements

1. Because many different groups use the financial statements of companies, they are sometimes referred to as "general-purpose" financial statements. The three primary financial statements are the balance sheet, the income statement, and the statement of cash flows.

The Balance Sheet

2. The balance sheet (or statement of financial position) provides a financial picture of a company's assets, liabilities, and owners' equity at a particular date. It helps external parties assess a company's liquidity and solvency.

3. Assets are economic resources that are owned or controlled by a company and are measurable in monetary terms.

4. Liabilities are the obligations of a company; they represent creditors' claims against the company's assets.

5. Owners' equity represents the remaining interest in the assets of an enterprise after the claims of creditors are satisfied.

6. Investments by owners, usually in the form of cash, increase owners' equity. If the business is a corporation, the amount invested by owners is often labeled stockholders' equity.

7. Owners' equity is decreased by distributions to owners. If the business is a corporation, distributions to owners (stockholders) are called dividends.

8. Owners' equity is also affected by the results of a company's operations—profits increase owners' equity, while losses decrease owners' eq-

uity. For a corporation, the amount of accumulated profits (or earnings) that have not been distributed to owners is called retained earnings, and this amount is added to capital stock to determine total owners' (stockholders') equity.

9. The balance sheet presents information based on the basic accounting equation—Assets = Liabilities + Owners' Equity.

10. Most companies prepare classified balance sheets, showing assets and liabilities subdivided into current and noncurrent categories. Also, balance sheets are usually presented on a comparative basis so that users can identify significant changes in a company's financial position from year to year.

11. The balance sheet has two primary limitations: (1) it does not reflect the current value of a business because items are reported at their historical costs, and (2) it reports only resources that can be measured in monetary terms.

The Income Statement

12. The income statement (or statement of earnings) shows the results of a company's operations over a period of time, usually a year. It summarizes a firm's revenues and expenses, thus helping investors and creditors assess an enterprise's profitability.

13. Revenues are increases in resources, primarily from the sale of goods or services.

14. Expenses are the costs incurred in normal business operations to generate revenues.

15. Net income (or net loss) is the overall measure of performance of a company's activities. It is equal to all revenues minus all expenses for the period. Net income increases owners' equity; net loss decreases owners' equity.

16. Comprehensive income is the number used to reflect an overall measure of the change in a company's wealth during the period. Comprehensive income includes items that, in general, arise from changes in market conditions unrelated to the business operations of a company.

17. In addition to revenues, expenses, and the resulting net income or loss, a corporation's income statement reports the amount of earnings per share (EPS), computed by dividing the net income (or loss) for the period by the number of shares of stock outstanding.

18. A corporation's income statement is often accompanied by a statement of retained earnings that reports the changes in retained earnings during a period.

The Statement of Cash Flows

19. The statement of cash flows is one of the three primary financial statements. This statement shows the cash inflows (receipts) and outflows (payments) of a company for a period of time. Cash flows are classified according to operating, investing, and financing activities.

How the Financial Statements Tie Together

20. The notion of "articulation" means that financial statements tie together, with certain figures in an operating statement helping to explain figures in comparative balance sheets.

Notes to the Financial Statements

21. The notes to the financial statements are considered an integral part of the statements. They provide vital information that cannot be captured solely by the reported dollar amounts in the financial statements.

22. The notes to financial statements are of four general types:

- summary of significant accounting policies
- additional information about the summary totals
- disclosure of information not recognized
- supplementary information

The External Audit

23. The audit report is a statement issued by an independent certified public accountant expressing an opinion concerning a company's financial statements. The audit report adds assurance that management's representations are not misleading, but it does not *guarantee* the accuracy of the statements. CPA firms perform credible audits to preserve their reputations and to avoid lawsuits.

Fundamental Concepts and Assumptions

25. Certain fundamental concepts and assumptions underlie the practice of accounting. They include the separate entity concept, the assumption of arm's-length transactions, the cost principle, the monetary measurement concept, the

going-concern assumption, and double-entry accounting.

COMMON ERRORS

The two most common problems students have with this chapter are:

1. Dealing with the new terms and the elements of the financial statements, which may be somewhat overwhelming at first glance.

2. Understanding how the financial statements relate to one another, that is, how they articulate.

---

1. New Terms

This chapter is an overview; the details will be explained carefully in subsequent chapters. Here you should concentrate on the general format and relationships of the primary financial statements: the balance sheet, the income statement, and the statement of cash flows.

2. Articulation of the Financial Statements

The relationship of the income statement to the balance sheet is sometimes confusing. Revenues less expenses equal net income, which is reported on the income statement. The amount of net income increases owners' equity. Net income therefore becomes a key element not only in the income statement, but also on the balance sheet, as part of the owners' equity section.

To illustrate this concept, assume that Simple Company has assets totaling $450,000; if its liabilities are $150,000, then owners' equity has to be $300,000. (Remember the basic accounting equation: Assets = Liabilities + Owners' Equity; therefore, $450,000 − $150,000 = $300,000.)

Recall that owners' equity has two main components: the amount contributed by owners and the amount earned and retained by the business (called retained earnings for a corporation). Thus, in the example, the $300,000 might consist of $100,000 contributed by the owners and $200,000 of retained earnings (the amount of earnings since the business began operations less any amounts paid back to owners in the form of dividends).

Continuing the illustration, assume that Simple Company has revenues of $750,000 and expenses of $525,000 during the next accounting period. Assets at the end of that period are $575,000 and liabilities remain at $150,000. During the period, the company distributes $100,000 to its stockholders in the form of a cash dividend. There is no change in the $100,000 of capital contributed by owners. What is the amount of retained earnings at the end of the accounting period? To determine the ending retained earnings, first compute net income ($750,000 revenues − $525,000 expenses = $225,000). The beginning retained earnings of $200,000 is increased by net income and decreased by the dividends. Therefore, the ending retained earnings balance is $325,000 ($200,000 + $225,000 − $100,000). We can see also that the accounting equation is still in balance at the end of the accounting period:

Assets = Liabilities + Owners' Equity

$575,000 = $150,000 + $425,000

$100,000 + $325,000

SELF-TEST

Matching

Instructions: Write the letter of each of the following terms in the space to the left of its appropriate definition.

a.	net income	**h.**	income statement
b.	liabilities	**i.**	retained earnings
c.	statement of cash flows	**j.**	owners' equity
d.	expenses	**k.**	assets
e.	comparative financial statements	**l.**	revenues
f.	balance sheet	**m.**	dividends
g.	primary financial statements	**n.**	going concern

_____ 1. Costs incurred in the normal course of business to generate revenues.

_____ 2. Financial statements prepared for two or more years.

_____ 3. The financial statement that shows the financial resources and claims against them, therefore showing the relationships of assets, liabilities, and owners' equity.

_____ 4. Economic resources that are owned or controlled by an enterprise.

_____ 5. A measure of the overall performance of a company, equal to all revenues minus all expenses for the period.

_____ 6. Obligations of an enterprise that represent creditors' claims against assets.

_____ 7. The accumulated portion of stockholders' equity that has been earned from profitable operations and has not been paid out in dividends.

_____ 8. Resource increases from the sale of goods or services during the normal operations of a business.

_____ 9. The financial statement that summarizes the revenues generated and the expenses incurred during a period.

_____ 10. The periodic distribution of earnings, usually in the form of cash, to the owners of the corporation.

_____ 11. The balance sheet, income statement, and statement of cash flows.

_____ 12. The ownership interest in an enterprise's assets; equals net assets (total assets minus total liabilities).

_____ 13. The financial statement showing cash inflows and outflows during a period.

_____ 14. The assumption that a business will continue to operate for the foreseeable future

True/False

Instructions: Place a check mark in the appropriate column to indicate whether each of the following statements is true or false.

	True	False
1. Some financial statements are called general-purpose statements because they are used by many groups of people for differing purposes.	_____	_____
. Transactions are always reported at current market values, even after the transaction date.	_____	_____
. Liquidity is a measure of long-term, debt-paying ability.	_____	_____
4. Profitability is directly related to an enterprise's ability to generate revenues in excess of expenses.	_____	_____
5. Assets are economic resources owned or controlled by a company.	_____	_____
6. For accounting purposes, an entity is the organizational unit for which accounting records are maintained.	_____	_____

		True	**False**
7.	Owners' equity fluctuates solely in relation to an entity's profitability.	_____	_____
8.	The basic accounting equation can be written as A – L = OE.	_____	_____
9.	The concept of net income encompasses revenues and expenses.	_____	_____
10.	The statement of cash flows is *not* one of the three primary financial statements.	_____	_____
11.	Revenues and expenses are listed on the balance sheet.	_____	_____
12.	The income statement is for a period of time, rather than for a particular date.	_____	_____
13.	Notes to financial statements are not needed to provide adequate disclosure of financial information.	_____	_____
14.	An independent CPA's audit report guarantees the accuracy of the financial statements.	_____	_____

Multiple Choice

Instructions: Circle the letter that best completes each of the following statements.

1. Which of the following is *not* one of the primary financial statements?

   a. The balance sheet
   b. The income statement
   c. The current year's budget
   d. The statement of cash flows

2. Which of the following is *not* a basic element of a balance sheet?

   a. Revenues
   b. Owners' equity
   c. Assets
   d. Liabilities

3. A balance sheet

   a. shows the relationships among assets, liabilities, and owners' equity.
   b. shows the relationships between revenues and expenses.
   c. is for a period of time.
   d. shows the current value of a business.

4. Which of the following would be classified as an asset?

   a. Notes payable
   b. Dividends
   c. Retained earnings
   d. Notes receivable

5. Which of the following would be classified as a liability?

   a. Accounts payable
   b. Inventory
   c. Cash
   d. Accounts receivable

6. Which of the following statements is *not* correct?

   a. Owners' equity represents a claim against assets.
   b. Owners' equity equals assets plus liabilities.
   c. Owners' equity represents the net assets of an entity.
   d. Owners' equity is a residual amount.

7. Owners' equity is decreased by

   a. operating profits.
   b. investments by owners.
   c. distributions to owners.
   d. sales of stock to investors.

8. The income statement

   a. shows the results of an enterprise's operations.
   b. lists revenues and expenses.
   c. measures profitability for a period of time.
   d. All of the above

9. Liquidity deals primarily with

   a. current assets and current liabilities.
   b. revenues and expenses.
   c. owners' equity.
   d. long-term debt.

10. Which of the following is *not* one of the three categories of cash flows reported on the statement of cash flows?

    a. Selling activities
    b. Investing activities
    c. Operating activities
    d. Financing activities

11. The concept of articulation means

    a. the financial statements are usually prepared on a comparative basis.
    b. accounting is considered more an art than a science.
    c. the statement of cash flows is based on the same data as the income statement and the balance sheet.
    d. the financial statements tie together, with operating statement items explaining or reconciling changes in major balance sheet categories.

12. Notes to financial statements are
    a. relatively unimportant.
    b. rarely included in a company's annual report to shareholders.
    c. an integral part of financial statements.
    d. an optional element of financial reporting.

13. The audit report included in the annual report to stockholders
    a. is prepared by internal accountants.
    b. is a professional opinion by an independent CPA.
    c. guarantees the accuracy of financial statements.
    d. does not add anything of value to financial statements.

14. Which of the following describes the characteristics of the accounting model?
    a. Separate entity
    b. Assumption of arm's-length transactions
    c. Going concern
    d. All of the above

15. Which of the following statements is *not* true?
    a. The balance sheet follows the accounting equation.
    b. The balance sheet shows the worth of a company.
    c. The balance sheet generally reports comparative information.
    d. None of the above statements are true.

Exercises

E2-1 Balance Sheet and Income Statement Items

Instructions: Indicate which of the following items are reported on the balance sheet and which are reported on the income statement. Also, indicate whether balance sheet items are assets (A), liabilities (L), or owners' equity (OE) items.

Item	Balance Sheet	Income Statement
Example: Notes Receivable	✓A	
1. Cash	_____	_____
2. Accounts Payable	_____	_____
3. Inventory	_____	_____
4. Revenues	_____	_____
5. Land	_____	_____
6. Expenses	_____	_____
7. Equipment	_____	_____
8. Mortgage Payable	_____	_____
9. Gains or Losses	_____	_____
10. Accounts Receivable	_____	_____
11. Retained Earnings	_____	_____
12. Supplies	_____	_____

E2-2   Balance Sheet Preparation

Instructions: Use the following data to prepare a balance sheet for IBC Company as of December 31, 2006.

Accounts Payable	$ 3,000
Accounts Receivable	4,500
Cash	2,000
Inventory	10,000
Notes Payable	12,500
Owners' Equity	?
Plant and Equipment	25,000

E2-3   Income Statement Preparation

Instructions: Use the following data to prepare an income statement for Office Supplies, Inc. for the year ended December 31, 2006.

Advertising Expense	$ 2,500
Sales Revenue	175,000
Cost of Goods Sold	100,000
Salaries Expense	20,000
Other Expenses	15,000
Income Taxes	18,000

1,000 shares of stock outstanding.

_____

_____

_____

_____

_____

_____

_____

_____

_____

_____

_____

_____

_____

_____

_____

_____

_____

_____

_____

_____

_____

_____

_____

E2-4   Owners' Equity Computations

Right Company had a beginning owners' equity balance of $64,500. Net income amounted to $12,750, and cash dividends paid during the year were $4,000.

1. What is the ending owners' equity balance?

2. If revenues were $45,000, what was the amount of expenses?

E2-5   Comparative Balance Sheet Relationships

The comparative balance sheets for Electronics Corporation are presented below.

Electronics Corporation
Balance Sheets
December 31, 2006 and 2005

Assets	2006	2005
Cash	$ 15,000	$ 12,000
Receivables	22,000	24,000
Inventory	54,000	51,000
Plant and equipment	105,000	100,000
Total assets	$196,000	$187,000

Liabilities and Owners' Equity	2006	2005
Accounts payable	$ 25,000	$ 32,000
Long-term debt	64,000	?
Owners' equity	107,000	81,000
Total liabilities and owners' equity	$196,000	$187,000

During 2006, the company incurred $29,000 of expenses and paid a cash dividend of $9,000.

1.   What is the total long-term debt as of December 31, 2005?

2.   What is the net income for 2006?

3.   What is the total revenue for 2006?

ANSWERS

Matching

1.	d	6.	b	11.	g
2.	e	7.	i	12.	j
3.	f	8.	l	13.	c
4.	k	9.	h	14.	n
5.	a	10.	m		

True/False

1.	T	6.	T	11.	F
2.	F	7.	F	12.	T
3.	F	8.	T	13.	F
4.	T	9.	T	14.	F
5.	T	10.	F		

Multiple Choice

1.	c	6.	b	11.	d
2.	a	7.	c	12.	c
3.	a	8.	d	13.	b
4.	d	9.	a	14.	d
5.	a	10.	a	15.	b

Exercises

E2-1   Balance Sheet and Income Statement Items

Item	Balance Sheet	Income Statement
1. Cash	✓A	
2. Accounts Payable	✓L	
3. Inventory	✓A	
4. Revenues		✓
5. Land	✓A	
6. Expenses		✓
7. Equipment	✓A	
8. Mortgage Payable	✓L	
9. Gains or Losses		✓
10. Accounts Receivable	✓A	
11. Retained Earnings	✓OE	
12. Supplies	✓A	

E2-2   Balance Sheet Preparation

IBC Company
Balance Sheet
December 31, 2006

Assets		Liabilities and Owners' Equity		
Cash	$ 2,000	Liabilities:		
Accounts receivable	4,500	Accounts payable	$ 3,000	
Inventory	10,000	Notes payable	12,500	
Plant and equipment	25,000	Total liabilities		$15,500
		Owners' equity		26,000*
Total assets	$41,500	Total liabilities and owners' equity		$41,500

* Assets = Liabilities + Owners' Equity
$41,500 = $15,500 + X
    X = $26,000

E2-3   Income Statement Preparation

Office Supplies, Inc.
Income Statement
For the Year Ended December 31, 2006

Sales revenue		$175,000
Expenses:		
Cost of goods sold	$100,000	
Advertising expense	2,500	
Salaries expense	20,000	
Other expenses	15,000	137,500
Income before taxes		$ 37,500
Income taxes		18,000
Net income		$ 19,500
EPS ($19,500/1,000)		$19.50

E2-4   Owners' Equity Computations

1. Beginning owners' equity	$64,500
Plus net income	12,750
	$77,250
Less cash dividends paid	4,000
Ending owners' equity	$73,250
2. Revenues	$45,000
Less expenses	32,250*
Net income	$12,750

*$45,000 – X = $12,750
          X = $32,250

E2-5   Comparative Balance Sheet Relationships

1. $32,000 + X (long-term debt) + $81,000 = $187,000
   X = $74,000

2. $81,000 + X (net income) − $9,000 = $107,000
   X = $35,000

3. X (revenues) − $29,000 = $35,000
   X = $64,000

Chapter 3
The Mechanics of Accounting

LEARNING OBJECTIVES

After studying this chapter, you should be able to:

1. Understand the process of transforming transaction data into useful accounting information.

2. Analyze transactions and determine how those transactions affect the accounting equation (Step One of the Accounting Cycle).

3. Record the effects of transactions using journal entries (Step Two of the Accounting Cycle).

4. Summarize the resulting journal entries through posting and prepare a trial balance (Step Three of the Accounting Cycle).

5. Describe how technology has affected the first three steps of the accounting cycle.

CHAPTER REVIEW

How Can We Collect All This Information?

1. Business transactions must be analyzed to determine how well an enterprise is managing its financial resources.

2. Business documents—such as invoices, check stubs, and other records—verify that transactions have occurred and provide objective evidence of the amounts involved.

3. By recording and summarizing transactions, the accounting cycle enables statement users to analyze the efficiency of business entities. This process transforms financial data into useful information.

4. The outputs of the accounting cycle are accounting reports based on the transactions of business entities.

How Do Transactions Affect the Accounting Equation?

5. The basic accounting equation (Assets = Liabilities + Owners' Equity) shows that a firm's resources are equal to the claims of creditors and owners against those resources.

6. The accounting equation must always remain in balance. An increase on one side of the equation must be exactly offset by a corresponding increase on the other side, or by a decrease on the same side.

7. Accounts provide an efficient way of categorizing transactions. Each account has two sides: debits are shown on the left side, and credits are shown on the right side.

8. A T-account is a simplified form of an account.

9. Debits and credits also refer to the increases and decreases in account balances that result from each transaction. As shown below, debits increase asset account balances and decrease liability and owners' equity account balances; the opposite is true for credits. You should memorize these important relationships.

Assets		=	Liabilities		+	Owners' Equity	
DR	CR		DR	CR		DR	CR
(+)	(−)		(−)	(+)		(−)	(+)

10. A major characteristic of the double-entry accounting system is that debits must always equal credits for each transaction.

11. Revenues increase owners' equity by increasing retained earnings, while expenses decrease owners' equity. Dividends, or other distributions to owners, also decrease owners' equity. The expanded accounting equation is shown in Exhibit 3–2 on page 89 of the textbook.

How Do We Record the Effects of Transactions?

12. Results of transactions are recorded first in chronological order in books of original entry called journals. Smaller companies use only a General Journal; larger companies may use special journals.

13. With a manual accounting system, the following format is used for journalizing transactions in a company's General Journal:

Date   Debit Entry.................. xxx

        Credit Entry............   xxx

       Explanation.

14. A company's transactions can be analyzed by examining the common elements of business activity, which include acquiring cash and other assets, using assets to produce products and services, collecting cash, and paying obligations and dividends.

15. For a corporation, dividends represent a return to stockholders of part of a company's earnings. The payment of dividends reduces retained earnings.

Posting Journal Entries and Preparing a Trial Balance

16. Results of transactions are classified by posting journal entries to accounts in the General Ledger. Each account has a title and a number that is specified in the company's chart of accounts.

17. At the end of a period, accounts are reviewed to determine their balances. A trial balance then lists all ledger account balances and checks to see if the total debits (on the left side of accounts) equal the total credits (on the right side of accounts).

Where Do Computers Fit In All This?

18. Computers facilitate the processing of data. They are fast and accurate. They greatly reduce the time required for posting entries, summarizing accounts, and determining account balances. Computers also assist in generating a variety of reports. However, computers still cannot think for themselves and have not replaced the need for analysis and human judgments in the accounting process.

COMMON ERRORS

The three most important, and sometimes most difficult, concepts to master in this chapter are:

1. The debit/credit, increase/decrease relationships of the accounts in the expanded accounting equation.

2. How to journalize transactions, giving proper recognition to the impact that each transaction has on the accounting equation.

3. The process of posting to ledger accounts.

1. Debits and Credits

The debit/credit, increase/decrease relationships often are difficult to learn, because most people tend to associate assets and revenues, the two "plus" categories—and liabilities, expenses, and dividends, the three "minus" categories. They think that because assets and revenues involve resources coming into a company, all such accounts would be treated the same way. In fact, they are treated in opposite ways. Assets are increased by debits and decreased by credits; revenues are increased by credits and decreased by debits. Similarly, liabilities are treated the opposite of expenses and dividends. Liabilities are increased by credits and decreased by debits; expenses and dividends are increased by debits and decreased by credits. Owners' equity, the remaining category, is increased by credits and decreased by debits; these accounts are treated in the same way as liabilities, since they are both on the same side of the accounting equation.

To help you understand the debit/credit, increase/decrease relationships of accounts, study the illustration of the expanded accounting equation on text page 89, which summarizes these important relationships. You should study these relationships until they become second nature to you. Remember, asset, expense, and dividend accounts are always increased by debits and decreased by credits; liability, owners' equity, and revenue accounts are always increased by credits and decreased by debits. The entire system of double-entry accounting is based on these relationships.

2. **Journalizing Transactions**

Once transactions are analyzed by looking at supporting business documents, they are journalized in books of original entry called journals. The format for making such entries is shown on page 90 of the text. In double-entry accounting, each recorded transaction must have equal debit and credit entries to the accounts, and the accounting equation must always stay in balance. You should review text pages 90–101 to see how various transactions are recorded and how they affect the accounting equation.

The three-step process for journal entries explained on page 99 should help you.

3. **Posting to the General Ledger**

Once journal entries are made, similar transactions are classified and summarized in the accounts through the posting process. The result of this process is that all transactions affecting cash are accumulated in the Cash account, and a balance for the total amount of cash available can be determined. The same is true for all other accounts. Exhibit 3–6 on text page 103 provides an illustration of this process and shows how the journal and the ledger are cross-referenced.

SELF-TEST

Matching

Instructions: Write the letter of each of the following terms in the space to the left of its appropriate definition.

a. account
b. credit
c. journal
d. chart of accounts
e. basic accounting equation
f. business documents
g. dividends

h. revenues
i. T-account
j. posting
k. ledger
l. debit
m. accounting cycle
n. trial balance

_____ 1. The means of transforming accounting data into accounting reports that can be interpreted and used in decision making.

_____ 2. An entry on the right side of an account.

_____ 3. A book or grouping of accounts in which data from recorded transactions are posted and thereby summarized.

_____ 4. A systematic listing of all accounts used by a company.

_____ 5. A distribution to stockholders of part of the earnings of a company.

_____ 6. A listing of all account balances; provides a means of testing whether total debits equal total credits for all accounts.

_____ 7. Assets equal liabilities plus owners' equity (A = L + OE).

_____ 8. The accounting record in which transactions are first entered; provides a chronological record of all business activities.

_____ 9. Records of transactions used as the basis for recording accounting entries.

_____ 10. The process of classifying, grouping, and recording similar transactions in common accounts by transferring amounts from the journal to the ledger.

_____ 11. Increases in resources from the sale of goods or services during the normal operations of a business.

_____ 12. An accounting record for classifying and accumulating the results of similar transactions; shows increases, decreases, and a balance.

_____ 13. An entry on the left side of an account.

_____ 14. A simplified depiction of an account in the form of the letter T.

True/False

Instructions: Place a check mark in the appropriate column to indicate whether each of the following statements is true or false.

	True	False
1. The accounting cycle facilitates transaction analysis through the recording and summarizing functions.	_____	_____
2. Inputs to the accounting process are transaction data as evidenced by business documents.	_____	_____
3. Debits (entries on the left side of accounts) increase asset, expense, and dividend accounts.	_____	_____
4. Credits (entries on the right side of accounts) decrease liability and owners' equity accounts.	_____	_____
5. The expanded accounting equation is Assets = Liabilities + Owners' Equity + (Revenues – Expenses – Dividends).	_____	_____

		True	**False**
6.	In using double-entry accounting, debits must always equal credits for the accounting equation to balance.	_____	_____
7.	Small businesses do *not* follow the same steps in their accounting cycles as large companies do.	_____	_____
8.	Ledgers are books of original entry.	_____	_____
9.	Entries are made in chronological order in the General Journal.	_____	_____
10.	Posting occurs before journalizing.	_____	_____
11.	The list of accounts used by a company is known as a chart of accounts.	_____	_____
12.	If the trial balance balances (that is, total debits equal total credits), there is complete assurance that the accounting records are correct.	_____	_____

Multiple Choice

Instructions: Circle the letter that best completes each of the following statements.

1. The basic inputs to the accounting process are

   a. economic indicators.
   b. transactions.
   c. managerial policies.
   d. computer tapes.

2. Outputs of the accounting process include

   a. general-purpose financial statements.
   b. government reports.
   c. managerial reports.
   d. All of the above

3. Which of the following functions is *not* a part of the accounting cycle?

   a. Auditing
   b. Analysis
   c. Reporting
   d. Summarizing

4. Which of the following is *not* a step in the accounting cycle?

   a. Analyzing transactions and business documents
   b. Journalizing and posting closing entries
   c. Preparing financial statements
   d. Selling goods or providing services

5. Which of the following is the correct sequence for the accounting cycle?

   a. Analyzing, journalizing, posting, adjusting entries, financial statements, closing entries
   b. Analyzing, posting, journalizing, financial statements, adjusting entries, closing entries
   c. Analyzing, journalizing, posting, financial statements, adjusting entries, closing entries
   d. None of the above

6. Which of the following items is least likely to be shown in a journal?

   a. The date of a transaction
   b. The accounts to be debited and credited
   c. The amounts to be debited and credited
   d. The source documents of a transaction

7. Which of the following statements is *not* true?

    a. Debits should always equal credits.
    b. Debits increase liability accounts.
    c. Debits increase asset accounts.
    d. Debits are always shown on the left side of an account.

8. If revenues exceed expenses during an accounting period and there are no distributions to owners

    a. total assets will be decreased.
    b. total owners' equity will be increased.
    c. total liabilities will be increased.
    d. None of the above

9. Expenses

    a. are increased by credits.
    b. are decreased by debits.
    c. increase owners' equity.
    d. decrease owners' equity.

10. When a company borrows money from a bank, the transaction

    a. increases assets and increases owners' equity.
    b. decreases assets and decreases liabilities.
    c. increases assets and increases liabilities.
    d. decreases assets and decreases owners' equity.

11. The issuance of stock by a company

    a. increases assets and increases liabilities.
    b. decreases assets and decreases liabilities.
    c. increases assets and increases owners' equity.
    d. decreases assets and increases owners' equity.

12. Revenue accounts

    a. have no effect on owners' equity.
    b. are increased by debits.
    c. usually have a debit balance.
    d. have the same debit/credit, increase/decrease relationship as owners' equity.

13. Which of the following is *not* true for expense accounts?

    a. They have the same debit/credit, increase/decrease relationship as assets.
    b. They are decreased by credits.
    c. They usually have a credit balance.
    d. They have the effect of decreasing owners' equity.

14. A trial balance

    a. is a formal statement presented to stockholders.
    b. lists all accounts with their appropriate balances.
    c. is an essential step in the accounting cycle.
    d. proves that all the journal entries have been made correctly.

15. Which of the following is *not* true for dividends?

    a. They are not liabilities until declared.
    b. They are net reductions in owners' equity.
    c. They are normal expenses of doing business.
    d. They reduce net assets.

16. Which of the following journal entries is probably *not* correct?

a. Cash   xxx
      Notes Payable   xxx
b. Inventory   xxx
      Cash   xxx
c. Cash   xxx
      Capital Stock   xxx
d. Rent Expense   xxx
      Interest Expense   xxx

17. Which of the following transactions would increase owners' equity?

a. Purchased inventory
b. Paid accounts payable
c. Sold goods at a profit
d. Sold goods at a loss

Exercises

E3-1   The Accounting Equation

Instructions: Indicate the effect of each of the following transactions on the accounting equation.

1. Purchased inventory on account

2. Borrowed money with a note

3. Sold goods (at a profit) on credit terms

4. Collected receivables

5. Paid debts (Accounts Payable)

6. Issued capital stock

7. Paid cash dividends

8. Purchased a building with a mortgage

9. Paid utilities

10. Purchased inventory for cash

E3-2   Decreasing an Account

Instructions: Indicate whether each of the following accounts is decreased by a debit or by a credit, and identify the normal balance of each account.

Account	Decreased by Debit or Credit	Normal Balance
Example: Equipment	Credit	Debit
1. Land		
2. Accounts Payable		
3. Capital Stock		
4. Notes Payable		
5. Accounts Receivable		
6. Inventory		
7. Retained Earnings		
8. Dividends		
9. Cash		
10. Mortgage Payable		

E3-3   Journalizing Transactions

Instructions: Using the form provided on page 29, journalize the following selected transactions for Airwise Corporation for January 2006.

Jan.   3   Issued 1,000 shares of stock for $10,000.
        5   Purchased equipment costing $3,500 for $500 cash and a note of $3,000.
        8   Purchased merchandise for $6,000 on account.
       10   Paid employee salaries of $1,500.
       15   Paid rent of $400.
       18   Sold merchandise that cost $2,000 for $3,500 on credit.
       24   Paid utilities of $150.
       29   Paid dividends of $5,000 to shareholders.

E3-4   Describing Journal Entries

Instructions: Describe a transaction that could have caused each of the following journal entries.

		Journal Entries			Transaction Descriptions
Jan.	1	Inventory	3,000		
		Accounts Payable		3,000	
	3	Accounts Receivable	5,000		
		Cost of Goods Sold	3,000		
		Sales Revenue		5,000	
		Inventory		3,000	
	10	Accounts Payable	3,000		
		Cash		3,000	
	12	Salaries Expense	2,000		
		Cash		2,000	
	17	Cash	5,000		
		Accounts Receivable		5,000	
	19	Rent Expense	1,000		
		Cash		1,000	

| JOURNAL | | | | PAGE | |
DATE	DESCRIPTION	POST. REF.	DEBIT		CREDIT

E3-5   Preparing a Trial Balance

Instructions: From the following list of accounts, prepare a trial balance. (Note: The amount in the Retained Earnings account must be calculated.)

Accounts Payable	$ 24,000
Sales Revenue	114,000
Equipment	55,000
Selling Expenses	60,000
Mortgage Payable	32,000
Land	85,000
Administrative Expenses	35,000
Accounts Receivable	13,000
Capital Stock	75,000
Cash	17,000
Retained Earnings	X
Inventory	28,000

Trial Balance

	Debits	Credits

ANSWERS

Matching

1.	m	6.	n	11.	h
2.	b	7.	e	12.	a
3.	k	8.	c	13.	l
4.	d	9.	f	14.	i
5.	g	10.	j		

True/False

1.	T	5.	T	9.	T
2.	T	6.	T	10.	F
3.	T	7.	F	11.	T
4.	F	8.	F	12.	F

Multiple Choice

1.	b	7.	b	13.	c
2.	d	8.	b	14.	b
3.	a	9.	d	15.	c
4.	d	10.	c	16.	d
5.	a	11.	c	17.	c
6.	d	12.	d		

Exercises

E3-1   The Accounting Equation

1. Increases assets (Inventory) and increases liabilities (Accounts Payable).
2. Increases assets (Cash) and increases liabilities (Notes Payable).
3. Decreases assets (Inventory), increases assets (Accounts Receivable), increases expenses (Cost of Goods Sold), and increases revenues (Sales Revenue).
4. Increases assets (Cash) and decreases assets (Accounts Receivable).
5. Decreases assets (Cash) and decreases liabilities (Accounts Payable).
6. Increases assets (Cash) and increases owners' equity (Capital Stock).
7. Decreases assets (Cash) and increases Dividends, which reduces Retained Earnings and therefore decreases owners' equity.
8. Increases assets (Building) and increases liabilities (Mortgage Payable).
9. Decreases assets (Cash) and increases expenses (Utilities Expense), which reduces Retained Earnings and therefore decreases owners' equity.
10. Increases assets (Inventory) and decreases assets (Cash).

E3-2   Decreasing an Account

Account		Decreased by Debit or Credit	Normal Balance
1.	Land	Credit	Debit
2.	Accounts Payable	Debit	Credit
3.	Capital Stock	Debit	Credit
4.	Notes Payable	Debit	Credit
5.	Accounts Receivable	Credit	Debit
6.	Inventory	Credit	Debit
7.	Retained Earnings	Debit	Credit
8.	Dividends	Credit	Debit
9.	Cash	Credit	Debit
10.	Mortgage Payable	Debit	Credit

E3-3   Journalizing Transactions

Jan.	3	Cash...	10,000	
		Capital Stock		10,000
		Issued 1,000 shares of stock for $10,000.		
	5	Equipment	3,500	
		Cash..		500
		Notes Payable...		3,000
		Purchased equipment costing $3,500 for $500 and a note of $3,000.		
	8	Inventory	6,000	
		Accounts Payable		6,000
		Purchased merchandise for $6,000 on account.		
	10	Salary Expense...	1,500	
		Cash..		1,500
		Paid employee salaries of $1,500.		
	15	Rent Expense..	400	
		Cash..		400
		Paid rent of $400.		
	18	Accounts Receivable..	3,500	
		Cost of Goods Sold	2,000	
		Sales Revenue		3,500
		Inventory		2,000
		Sold merchandise costing $2,000 for $3,500 on credit.		
	24	Utilities Expense	150	
		Cash..		150
		Paid utilities of $150.		
	29	Dividends	5,000	
		Cash..		5,000
		Paid cash dividends of $5,000 to shareholders.		

E3-4   Describing Journal Entries

Jan.	1	Purchased inventory on credit for $3,000.
	3	Sold merchandise costing $3,000 for $5,000 on credit.
	10	Paid accounts payable of $3,000.
	12	Paid salary expense of $2,000.
	17	Collected accounts receivable of $5,000.
	19	Paid rent of $1,000.

E3-5   Preparing a Trial Balance

	Debits	Credits
Cash	$ 17,000	
Accounts Receivable	13,000	
Inventory	28,000	
Equipment	55,000	
Land	85,000	
Accounts Payable		$ 24,000
Mortgage Payable		32,000
Capital Stock		75,000
Retained Earnings		48,000*
Sales Revenue		114,000
Selling Expenses	60,000	
Administrative Expenses	35,000	
Totals	$293,000	$293,000

*$293,000 = $245,000 (total of other credits) + X (Retained Earnings)
X = $48,000

Chapter 4
Completing the Accounting Cycle

LEARNING OBJECTIVES

After studying this chapter, you should be able to:

1. Describe how accrual accounting allows for timely reporting and a better measure of a company's economic performance.

2. Explain the need for adjusting entries and make adjusting entries for unrecorded receivables, unrecorded liabilities, prepaid expenses, and unearned revenues.

3. Explain the preparation of the financial statements, the explanatory notes, and the audit report.

4. Complete the closing process in the accounting cycle.

5. Understand how all the steps in the accounting cycle fit together.

EXPANDED MATERIAL LEARNING OBJECTIVE

6. Make adjusting entries for prepaid expenses and unearned revenues when the original cash amounts are recorded as expenses or revenues instead of as assets or liabilities.

CHAPTER REVIEW

Accrual Accounting

1. The accounting model assumes the need for periodic reporting and accrual accounting.

2. The time period concept states that an accounting entity's total life may be divided into distinct periods for reporting accounting information on a timely basis. Most companies use a 12-month reporting period.

3. A calendar year is a 12-month period ending December 31. If the 12-month accounting period ends on any day of the year other than December 31, it is called a fiscal year.

4. Cash-basis accounting recognizes revenues and expenses only when cash is received or paid.

5. Accrual-basis accounting recognizes revenues and expenses when they are earned or incurred regardless of when cash is received or paid. For measuring income for most business entities, accrual-basis accounting is more appropriate than cash-basis accounting. Accrual-basis accounting is required by GAAP.

6. Because the life of a business is divided into reporting periods, accountants must use estimates and judgments in assigning the revenues and expenses to different accounting periods and in measuring assets and liabilities.

7. In measuring income on an accrual basis, only those revenues that actually have been earned during a period are reported. This is called the *revenue recognition principle*.

8. Two criteria must be met in recognizing revenues: (a) the earnings process must be substantially complete, and (b) cash has either been collected, or collectibility is reasonably assured.

9. The *matching principle* states that all expenses incurred to generate revenues should be reported in the same accounting period as the revenues.

10. Under accrual-basis accounting, net income is determined by subtracting matched expenses from the revenues recognized during an accounting period.

11. Accrual-basis accounting is necessary not only for determining net income but also for reporting proper balance sheet amounts at year-end.

Adjusting Entries

12. Adjusting entries usually are required at the end of each accounting period to report all asset, liability, and owners' equity account balances properly and to recognize all revenues and expenses for the period on an accrual basis.

13. The areas most commonly requiring analysis to see if adjusting entries are needed are unrecorded receivables, unrecorded liabilities, prepaid expenses, and unearned revenues.

14. Preparing adjusting entries involves two steps: (1) determine whether the amounts recorded for all assets, liabilities, and owners' equity accounts are correct (fix the balance sheet) and (2) determine whether revenues and expenses are reported correctly (fix the income statement).

15. T-accounts are useful in analyzing adjusting entries. Two illustrations are provided.

    a. Monthly wages are paid on the 15th of each month. At December 31, $1,500 of wages have been incurred and will be paid next January 15th. Assuming a December 31 year-end, what adjusting entry should be made?

    Answer:

    Wages Expense 1,500

        Wages Payable   1,500

    Analysis:

	Wages Expense	**Wages Payable**
Original entry	none	none
Adjusting entry	1,500	1,500
Updated balance	1,500	1,500
	To income statement	To balance sheet

    b. On July 1, $300 is paid for a 3-year insurance premium. The cash payment is re-

corded as Prepaid Insurance. Assuming a December 31 year-end, what adjusting entry should be made?

Answer:

Insurance Expense............   50

    Prepaid Insurance   50

($300 ÷ 3 years = $100; $100 × 1/2 year = $50)

Analysis:

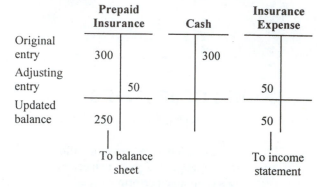

	Prepaid Insurance	**Cash**	**Insurance Expense**
Original entry	300	300	
Adjusting entry	50		50
Updated balance	250		50
	To balance sheet		To income statement

Preparing Financial Statements

16. When all transactions have been analyzed, journalized, and posted to the ledger accounts, and when all adjusting entries have been made, the accounts can be summarized and presented in the form of financial statements.

17. The notes to the financial statements are an integral part of the statements. The notes describe the assumptions made and methods used in preparing the statements. They also provide additional detail about specific items.

18. An audit is generally conducted by independent accountants (CPAs) to add credibility and assurance that the financial statements have been prepared in conformity with generally accepted accounting principles.

Closing the Books

19. *Real accounts* are those that are not closed to a zero balance at the end of each accounting period. They are permanent accounts appearing on the balance sheet.

20. *Nominal accounts* are temporary in that they are reduced to a zero balance through the closing process at the end of each accounting period. They are used to accumulate and classify all revenue and expense items for the period.

21. Closing entries reduce all nominal accounts to a zero balance, making the accounting records ready for a new cycle of transactions. Without

closing entries, revenue and expense balances would extend from period to period, which would make it difficult to separate the operating results of each accounting period.

22. Revenue accounts are closed by being debited; expense accounts are closed by being credited. For a corporation, the difference between total revenues and total expenses (net income or loss) is debited or credited to Retained Earnings.

23. In a corporation, the Dividends account is a temporary account and is closed directly to Retained Earnings by being credited.

24. The last step in the accounting cycle (an optional one) is to balance the accounts and to prepare a post-closing trial balance, which lists all real account balances. This step, which is performed prior to the start of a new cycle, provides some assurance that the previous steps in the cycle have been performed properly.

EXPANDED MATERIAL

Adjusting Entries: Original Entries to Expense or Revenue Accounts

25. Two methods for recording prepaid expenses are the asset approach and the expense approach. If adjusting entries are made correctly, the result will be identical regardless of which approach is used.

26. The liability approach and the revenue approach are two different methods for recording unearned revenues. Both approaches produce the same result if adjusting entries are made correctly.

COMMON ERRORS

The major difficulty in this chapter is in making adjusting entries for prepaid expenses and unearned revenues. Unrecorded receivables and liabilities are easier to see, since earned revenues that have not been previously recorded obviously need to be recorded. Similarly, if expenses have been incurred but not yet recorded, they must be entered into the accounting records if the financial statements are to be reported accurately.

The problem with prepaid expenses and unearned revenues is that you must determine what entry was made originally in order to make the appropriate adjusting entry, so that the ending balances will be brought current. A related problem is knowing which accounts go together, that is, which are the proper

"companion" accounts. Another difficulty for some students is understanding the closing process.

1. **Prepaid Expenses**

When cash is paid, the Cash account is credited to reduce it, but what is debited? A common practice is to debit a Prepaid Expense account (an asset), showing that cash was paid for an asset having future benefit to the company. If an asset account is debited initially, the year-end adjustment records the amount of service potential that has been used up from that asset, that is, the amount of expense. This is done by debiting the expense account and crediting the prepaid asset account.

To illustrate, if a company pays $3,600 for one year's rent in advance, it might debit Prepaid Rent and credit Cash. At year-end Prepaid Rent would be credited (reduced) and the companion account—Rent Expense—would be debited to show the amount of expense for that period.

2. **Unearned Revenues**

To illustrate adjusting entries for unearned revenues, assume that on July 1 a company received $2,400 cash in advance for services to be rendered over the next 12 months. At year-end (December 31), $1,200 must be recognized as revenue and $1,200 as a liability (for unearned revenue). First you must determine what original entry was made upon the receipt of the cash. Obviously, the Cash account was debited (increased), but what was credited? If Unearned Service Revenue (a liability) was credited originally, then the adjusting entry must debit the liability (to reduce it) and credit the companion or related account—Service Revenue—to increase it to the proper amount that has been earned by the end of the accounting period. Thus, the companion accounts are Unearned Service Revenue (a liability) and Service Revenue (a revenue). If the liability account is originally credited when cash is received, at year-end it must be reduced and the revenue account increased.

3. **Closing Process**

To understand the closing process, you must first distinguish between real, or permanent, accounts and nominal, or temporary, accounts. All income statement accounts are nominal accounts. Dividends also is a temporary account. All temporary accounts must be closed to a zero balance at the end of an accounting period, so that the amounts will not be carried over into the next period. Since the totals in these accounts reflect the results of operations *during* a period of time, it is important that only relevant amounts be counted in that period. If nominal accounts were cumulative, financial statement readers would have no way of judging the results of a company's operations during a period, or of comparing one period with the next.

All balance sheet accounts are real accounts and are not closed at the end of an accounting period. This is because they represent a company's cumulative financial status as of a point in time. If balance sheet accounts were closed, then long-term assets, for example, would be underrepresented. Land purchased for $50,000 in 2001, for example, would not be shown on the balance sheet, even though it still had future benefit to the company.

Thus revenue, expense, and dividend accounts are closed at the end of each accounting period, while asset, liability, and owners' equity accounts (including Retained Earnings) remain open. Since revenue accounts normally have credit balances, they are closed by being debited; expenses and dividends normally have debit balances, so they are closed by being credited. These accounts may be closed directly to Retained Earnings.

SELF-TEST

Matching

Instructions: Write the letter of each of the following terms in the space to the left of its appropriate definition.

a. fiscal year
b. accrual-basis accounting
c. time period concept
d. closing entries
e. unearned revenues
f. calendar year

g. real accounts
h. adjusting entries
i. post-closing trial balance
j. nominal accounts
k. cash-basis accounting
l. prepaid expenses

_____ 1. A system of accounting in which transactions are recorded, and revenues and expenses are recognized, only when cash is received or paid.

_____ 2. The idea that the life of a business is divided into distinct and relatively short time periods so that accounting information can be timely.

_____ 3. A listing of all real account balances after the closing process has been completed.

_____ 4. Amounts received in advance of the actual earnings process.

_____ 5. Entries that reduce all nominal, or temporary, accounts to a zero balance at the end of each accounting period, transferring their balances to a permanent balance sheet account.

_____ 6. An entity's reporting year, covering 12 months ending on December 31.

_____ 7. Permanent accounts that are not closed to a zero balance at the end of each accounting period.

_____ 8. Payments in advance for items normally charged to expense at a later date.

_____ 9. An entity's reporting year, covering a 12-month accounting period and ending at the end of a month other than December.

_____ 10. Temporary accounts that are closed to a zero balance at the end of each accounting period.

_____ 11. A system of accounting in which revenues and expenses are recorded as they are earned and incurred, not necessarily when cash is received or paid.

_____ 12. Entries required in accrual-basis accounting at the end of each accounting period to recognize all revenues and expenses for the period and to report proper amounts for asset, liability, and owners' equity accounts.

True/False

Instructions: Place a check mark in the appropriate column to indicate whether each of the following statements is true or false.

	True	False
1. The going concern assumption states that it is important to report accounting information on a timely basis.	F	
2. The life of a business enterprise is divided into distinct accounting periods because users need timely information to make ongoing economic decisions.	T	
3. A company that closes its books on December 31 of each year is said to report on a fiscal year.	F	
4. Most corporations issue an annual report that includes the primary financial statements.	T	
5. When the life of a business enterprise is divided into distinct accounting periods, estimates and judgments are required in measuring financial information.	T	
6. Accrual-basis accounting recognizes revenues only when the company collects cash.	F	

		True	**False**
7.	Over the life of an enterprise, cash-basis accounting and accrual-basis accounting measure the same amount of net income.	T	
8.	An independent audit guarantees the accuracy of financial statements.	F	
9.	According to the matching principle, expenses are matched with revenues in the accounting period in which they are paid.	F	
10.	Net income, as measured by accrual accounting, is the difference between cash receipts and cash disbursements.	F	
11.	Source documents signal the need for adjusting entries to be made at the end of each accounting period.	F	
12.	Unrecorded receivables and unrecorded liabilities generally do *not* require adjusting entries.	F	
13.	Adjusting entries must be journalized and posted just as other entries must be..........	T	
14.	At the end of every accounting period, liability accounts are closed by being debited.	F	
15.	Expense accounts are closed by being credited.	T	
16.	Dividends are closed directly to Retained Earnings.	T	
17.	A post-closing trial balance lists only real accounts.	T	

Multiple Choice

Instructions: Circle the letter that best completes each of the following statements.

1. Which of the following is *not* a characteristic of the accounting model?
   a. The accounting entity is considered a separate and distinct economic unit
   b. Arm's-length transactions provide the basis for accounting entries
   c. The cash basis of accounting
   d. The necessity of periodic reporting

2. A fiscal-year accounting period
   a. covers 12 months and usually ends on the last day of a month other than December 31.
   b. covers 12 months and always ends on December 31.
   c. is always the same as the calendar year.
   d. is set by a company's board of directors and usually lasts for more than a year.

3. Accrual-basis accounting
   a. recognizes revenues only when cash is received.
   b. recognizes revenues when they are earned.
   c. is used by all businesses.
   d. eliminates the need to divide the life of a business into reporting periods.

4. Revenues *usually* should be recognized when
   a. goods are manufactured.
   b. a sale is made and goods are delivered.
   c. orders for merchandise are placed.
   d. cash is collected.

5. Which of the following accounts would *not* normally require an adjusting entry at the end of an accounting period?

   a. Prepaid Insurance
   b. Unearned Service Revenue
   c. Salaries Payable
   d. Land

6. When are adjusting entries generally made?

   a. After taking a post-closing trial balance
   b. At year-end before the financial statements are prepared
   c. At year-end after the financial statements are prepared
   d. After closing entries are made

7. Salaries expense incurred but not yet recorded is an example of a(n)

   a. unrecorded receivable.
   b. unrecorded liability.
   c. prepaid expense.
   d. unearned revenue.

8. If a company pays a 2-year insurance premium in advance and initially debits Prepaid Insurance to record the transaction, the adjusting entry at the end of the accounting period will contain a

   a. credit to Insurance Expense.
   b. credit to Insurance Payable.
   c. credit to Prepaid Insurance.
   d. credit to Cash.

9. If a company at year-end has not yet paid its employees their salaries for the last month of the year, the adjusting entry should contain a

   a. credit to Salaries Payable.
   b. credit to Cash.
   c. credit to Salary Expense.
   d. credit to Retained Earnings.

10. If a company at year-end has paid its rent for the following year but no entry has been made to record the transaction, an adjusting entry should contain a

   a. debit to Prepaid Rent.
   b. debit to Cash.
   c. debit to Rent Expense.
   d. debit to Retained Earnings.

11. If a company initially credits Rent Received in Advance to record rent payments received for the last 2 months of the current year and 10 months of the next year, the adjusting entry at year-end will include a

   a. debit to Rent Received in Advance.
   b. debit to Cash.
   c. debit to Rent Revenue.
   d. debit to Rent Receivable.

12. Which of the following accounts is *not* likely to be involved in an adjusting entry?

    a. Prepaid Insurance
    b. Rent Received in Advance
    c. Salaries Payable
    d. Cash

13. An audit generally will *not* include

    a. reviewing adjustments.
    b. reviewing the accounting system.
    c. verifying cash balances.
    d. verifying all account balances.

14. Which of the following accounts is *not* a temporary account?

    a. Utilities Expense
    b. Supplies on Hand
    c. Sales Revenue
    d. Dividends

15. Which of the following accounts is closed to a zero balance at the end of an accounting period?

    a. Land
    b. Retained Earnings
    c. Accounts Payable
    d. Interest Expense

16. Which of the following accounts is a permanent account?

    a. Sales Revenue
    b. Salaries Payable
    c. Cost of Goods Sold
    d. Insurance Expense

17. Which of the following types of accounts are closed to Retained Earnings at the end of an accounting period?

    a. Asset and liability accounts
    b. Revenue and liability accounts
    c. Revenue and expense accounts
    d. Asset and expense accounts

18. Closing entries

    a. are made only when an entity goes out of business.
    b. must be journalized and posted just like other accounting entries.
    c. adjust only revenue and expense accounts to the proper balances at the end of each accounting period.
    d. are usually made at the close of each business day.

19. Which of the following accounts will *not* appear on a post-closing trial balance?

    a. Dividends
    b. Retained Earnings
    c. Dividends Payable
    d. Accounts Payable

Exercises

E4-1   Adjusting Entries

Precision Company's accountant discovered the following items in examining the accounting records shortly after year-end.

1. Company employees earned $2,000 in salaries for the month of December, but they have not been paid. No entry has been made to record the accrual.

2. The company, on the first day of its fiscal year, paid a $3,000 insurance premium. This premium covers the current year as well as the next two years. Prepaid Insurance was debited and Cash credited to record the transaction.

3. The company billed a client $10,000 for services performed. Payment has not yet been received. No entry has been made to record the earned revenue.

4. The company borrowed $100,000 from the bank on the first day of the fiscal year. Interest at 12 percent is payable annually on the note, which matures in three years.

Instructions: Prepare the necessary adjusting entries. (Omit explanations.)

DATE	DESCRIPTION	POST. REF.	DEBIT	CREDIT

JOURNAL   PAGE

E4-2   Adjusting Entries

The unadjusted trial balance for Cross Town Inc. on December 31, 2006, includes the following account balances.

Cash	$12,500
Prepaid Rent	3,000
Unearned Service Revenues	1,025

A review of the company records reveals the following pertinent data:

1. On March 1, 2006, the company paid one year's rent in advance at $250 per month.

2. During the year, Cross Town received cash for services to be performed in the future. At year-end, the company had not performed services worth $700.

Instructions: Complete the T-accounts and make the appropriate adjusting entries for each situation as of December 31, 2006.

	Prepaid Rent	Cash	Rent Expense
Original entry.............................			
Adjusting entry			
Updated balance			
	To balance sheet (Asset)		To income statement (Expense)

	Unearned Service Revenues	Cash	Service Revenues
Original entry.............................			
Adjusting entry			
Updated balance			
	To balance sheet (Liability)		To income statement (Revenue)

JOURNAL   **PAGE**

DATE	DESCRIPTION	POST. REF.	DEBIT	CREDIT

E4-3   Closing Entry

Instructions: Based on the following account balances, taken from the adjusted trial balance of Pitch & Hit Company, prepare the closing entry at the end of the accounting period.

Cash	$ 1,500
Accounts Receivable	2,200
Inventory	15,400
Land	28,000
Accounts Payable	700
Mortgage Payable	18,000
Capital Stock	20,000
Retained Earnings (Beginning)	8,400
Sales Revenue	49,000
Cost of Goods Sold	24,800
Selling Expenses	11,500
General and Administrative Expenses	5,600
Dividends	2,000

JOURNAL   PAGE

DATE	DESCRIPTION	POST. REF.	DEBIT	CREDIT

ANSWERS

Matching

1.	k	5.	d	9.	a
2.	c	6.	f	10.	j
3.	i	7.	g	11.	b
4.	e	8.	l	12.	h

True/False

1.	F	7.	T	13.	T
2.	T	8.	F	14.	F
3.	F	9.	F	15.	T
4.	T	10.	F	16.	T
5.	T	11.	F	17.	T
6.	F	12.	F		

Multiple Choice

1.	c	8.	c	14.	b
2.	a	9.	a	15.	d
3.	b	10.	a	16.	b
4.	b	11.	a	17.	c
5.	d	12.	d	18.	b
6.	b	13.	d	19.	a
7.	b				

Exercises

E4-1   Adjusting Entries

1. Salary Expense............................. 2,000
      Salaries Payable   2,000

2. Insurance Expense.......................... 1,000
      Prepaid Insurance   1,000
   ($3,000 ÷ 3 = $1,000 per year)

3. Accounts Receivable....................... 10,000
      Service Revenues   10,000

4. Interest Expense 12,000
      Interest Payable   12,000
   ($100,000 × 0.12 × 1 year = $12,000)

E4-2   Adjusting Entries

1. Rent Expense.................................. 2,500
      Prepaid Rent   2,500
   To recognize 10 months' rent ex-
   pense at $250 per month and show
   2 months' prepaid rent applicable
   to next period.

	Prepaid Rent		Cash		Rent Expense	
Original entry.............................	3,000			3,000		
Adjusting entry		2,500			2,500	
Updated balance	500				2,500	

To balance sheet	To income statement
(Asset)	(Expense)

2. Unearned Service Revenues............   325
        Service Revenues   325
    *To adjust the liability for unearned
    service revenues received in ad-
    vance and to recognize partial
    earning of service revenues.*

	Unearned Service Revenues		Cash		Service Revenues	
Original entry...............................		1,025	1,025			
Adjusting entry	325					325
Updated balance		700				325

To balance sheet	To income statement
(Liability)	(Revenue)

E4-3   Closing Entry

Sales Revenue...	49,000	
Cost of Goods Sold....................................		24,800
Selling Expenses.......................................		11,500
General and Administrative Expenses		5,600
Dividends...		2,000
Retained Earnings.....................................		5,100

Chapter 5
Introduction to Financial Statement Analysis

LEARNING OBJECTIVES

After studying this chapter, you should be able to:

1. Explain the purpose of financial statement analysis.

2. Understand the relationships between financial statement numbers and use ratios in analyzing and describing a company's performance.

3. Use common-size financial statements to perform comparison of financial statements across years and between companies.

4. Understand the DuPont framework and how return on equity can be decomposed into its profitability, efficiency, and leverage components.

5. Use cash flow information to evaluate cash flow ratios.

6. Understand the limitations of financial statement analysis.

CHAPTER REVIEW

Financial Statement Analysis

1. Financial statements are analyzed to detect signs of existing deficiencies and to predict future performance. Financial statement analysis involves examination of key relationships among financial statement numbers (called financial ratios) and trends in those relationships. It is important to compare ratios against past years and to values for other companies in the same industry rather than to rely on absolute values.

2. Financial statement analysis examines both the relationships among financial statement numbers and the trends in those numbers over time.

3. Relationships between financial statement amounts are called financial ratios.

4. Management uses the analysis to help in making operating, investing, and financing decisions; and investors and creditors analyze financial statements to decide whether to invest in, or loan money to, a company.

5. The usefulness of financial ratios is greatly enhances when they are compared with past values and with values for other firms in the same industry.

6. Financial statement analysis helps users of financial statements to better predict how the company will do in the future.

Financial Statement Number Relationships

7. Relationships between financial statement amounts, called financial ratios, help illustrate trends within companies.

8. Debt ratio is computed as total liabilities divided by total assets. Debt ratio indicates the extent to which a company has borrowed money to leverage the owners' investments and increase the size of the company.

9. Current ratio is computed as total current assets divided by total current liabilities. Current ratio provides users with information regarding liquidity, or the company's ability to pay its debts in the short run.

10. Return on sales is computed as net income divided by sales. Return on sales indicates how many pennies of profit a company makes on each dollar of sales.

11. Asset turnover is computed as sales divided by total assets. Asset turnover indicates how many dollars of sales a company generates on each dollar in assets.

12. Return on equity is computed as net income divided by total stockholders' equity. Return on equity indicates how many cents of profit were earned for each dollar of stockholder investment.

13. Price-earnings (PE) ratio is computed as the market value of the total shares outstanding divided by net income. Price-earnings ratio indicates the amount investors are willing to pay for each dollar of earnings, and it is an indication of a company's growth potential.

Common-Size Financial Statement

14. Common-size financial statements are a quick and easy way to provide additional insight into the financial relationships of the elements reported in the financial statements. With common-size statements, all amounts for a given year are reported as a percentage of a base amount, generally total revenue for the year.

15. As a sales for a company grows, other numbers, such as total assets and expenses, become more difficult to compare directly from year to year. Common-size financial statements help solve this comparability problem.

16. Common-size financial statements are prepared by dividing all financial statement numbers for a given year by sales for the same year.

17. By comparing the percentages for financial statement numbers from year to year, users can discover trends in the performance of a company.

18. A common-size income statement indicates the number of pennies of each expense for each dollar of sales.

19. The asset section of a common-size balance sheet indicates how efficiently a company uses its assets compared with prior years.

20. Common-size financial statements do not provide all necessary decision-making information, but they do provide users with good questions to ask about trends in a company.

DuPont Framework

21. The DuPont framework provides a systematic approach to identifying the key elements contributing to a company's return on equity (ROE). ROE can be decomposed as follows:

Return on Equity = Profitability × Efficiency × Leverage

ROE = Profit Margin × Asset Turnover × Assets-To-Equity Ratio

$$\text{ROE} = \frac{\text{Net Income}}{\text{Revenues}} \times \frac{\text{Revenues}}{\text{Assets}} \times \frac{\text{Assets}}{\text{Equity}}$$

Profit margin, also known as return on sales, indicates the number of pennies in profit generated from each dollar of sales. Asset turnover indicates the number of dollars in sales generated by each dollar of assets. Assets-to-equity ratio indicates the number of dollars of assets acquired for each dollar invested by stockholders.

22. If a DuPont analysis suggests problems in any of the three return-on-equity (ROE) components additional ratios in each area can shed more light on the exact nature of the problem.

Cash Flow Ratios

23. Analysis of cash flow information is important in those situations in which net income does not give an accurate picture of the economic performance off a company. When a company has large noncash expenses (such as write-offs and depreciation), rapid growth, or hopes to "dress up the numbers" for an important event, cash flow information provides users with additional useful information regarding the financial health of a company.

24. Cash flow-to-net income ratio is computed as cash flow from operations divided by net income. Cash flow-to-net income ratio indicates the extent to which accrual accounting assumptions and adjustments have been included in computing net income.

25. Cash flow adequacy ratio is computed as cash from operations divided by expenditures for fixed asset additions and acquisitions of new businesses. Cash flow adequacy ratio indicates how easily a company meets its investment requirements with cash generated through the normal course of business. A company with a high cash flow adequacy ratio is sometimes referred to as a "cash cow."

Limitations

26. Financial statement analysis usually does not provide answers but rather points in directions where further investigation is needed. Financial statements do not provide all the information about the overall health of a company, and historical financial statements are not always as useful as press releases and other current news available for a company. Another limitation of financial statement analysis is the lack of comparability between different companies' accounting assumptions.

COMMON ERRORS

The most common problems students have with this chapter are:

1. Computing and understanding financial ratios.

2. Understanding how the different parts of the DuPont Framework contribute to a company's return on equity.

1. Financial Ratios

The financial ratios introduced in this chapter are quite common in financial statement analysis. Debt ratio is computed as total liabilities divided by total assets and represents the percentage of assets that were bought through borrowing. Current ratio is computed as total current assets divided by total current liabilities and represents how many dollars of current assets a company has for each dollar of current liabilities. Return on sales is computed as net income divided by sales and represents the number of pennies of profit earned on each dollar of sales. Asset turnover is computed as sales divided by total assets and represents how much a company generates in sales for each dollar of assets. Return on equity is computed as net income divided by stockholders' equity and represents how many pennies of profit were earned for each dollar of stockholder investment. Price-earnings ratio is computed as market value of shares outstanding divided by net income and represents the amount investors are willing to pay for each dollar of earnings.

2. DuPont Framework

Return on equity indicates the profit earned for each dollar of stockholder investment. Under the DuPont framework, three ratios contribute to a company's return on equity. These three ratios are return on sales (a measure of profitability), asset turnover (a measure of efficiency), and assets-to-equity ratio (a measure of leverage). To compute return on

equity, multiply these three ratios together. An increase (or decrease) in any of these three ratios causes an increase (or decrease) in the firm's return on equity. Intuitively, this relationship between the components and the overall return on equity makes sense if one considers each component separately. If a company's profitability (as measured by return on sales) increases, the stockholders will receive more return on their investment. If a company's efficiency (as measured by asset turnover) increases, the company will earn more money on its existing assets, and the stockholders will receive more return on their investment. If a company's leverage (as measured by the assets-to-equity ratio) increases, the company has a lower proportion of equity, and there are less stockholders to share in the profits, so there is a greater return per stockholder.

SELF-TEST

Matching

Instructions: Write the letter of each of the following terms in the space to the left of its appropriate definition

a.	common-size financial statements	**g.**	financial statement analysis
b.	return on equity	**h.**	current ratio
c.	DuPont framework	**i.**	asset turnover
d.	financial ratios	**j.**	cash flow adequacy ratio
e.	debt ratio	**k.**	liquidity
f.	cash flow-to-net income ratio	**l.**	price-earnings ratio

_____ 1. A company's ability to pay its debts in the short run.

_____ 2. Relationships among financial statement amounts.

_____ 3. The relationship of net income to stockholders' equity.

_____ 4. The relationship of market value of shares outstanding to net income

_____ 5. The relationship of total liabilities to total assets.

_____ 6. The relationship of cash from operations to expenditures for fixed asset additions and acquisitions of new businesses.

_____ 7. The relationship of cash flow to net income.

_____ 8. The relationship of current assets to current liabilities.

_____ 9. Statements with all amounts for a given year being shown as a percentage of sales for that year.

_____ 10. A systematic approach to identifying general factors causing return on equity to deviate from normal.

_____ 11. The relationship of sales to total assets.

_____ 12. The examination of both the relationships among financial statement numbers and the trends in those numbers over time.

True/False

Instructions: Place a check mark in the appropriate column to indicate whether each of the following statements is true or false.

	True	**False**
1. Financial statement analysis helps identify deficiencies and future potential for company performance.	_____	_____
2. Current ratio is a common measurement of a company's profitability.	_____	_____
3. Relationships between financial statement amounts are called financial ratios.	_____	_____
4. Asset turnover is a common measurement of a company's efficiency.	_____	_____
5. Common-size financial statements are usually the most sophisticated analytical tool available.	_____	_____
6. Cash flow ratios are more commonly used than the DuPont framework.	_____	_____
7. Price-earnings ratio is an indication of a company's growth potential.	_____	_____
8. Assets-to-equity ratio is a common measurement of a company's leverage.	_____	_____
9. A common-size income statement can be used to pinpoint exactly which expenses are causing a company's profitability to increase or decrease.	_____	_____
10. Debt ratio is computed as total assets divided by total liabilities.	_____	_____

	True	False
11. The informativeness of financial ratios is greatly enhanced when they are compared with past values and with values for other firms in the same industry.	_____	_____
12. Common-size financial statements are always computed as a percentage of sales. ...	_____	_____
13. Much decision-relevant information is contained outside the company's financial statements.	_____	_____
14. Return on sales indicates how pennies of profit a company makes on each dollar of sales..	_____	_____
15. Price-earnings ratio is a component of the DuPont framework.	_____	_____

Multiple Choice

Instructions: Circle the letter that best completes each of the following statements.

1. Relationships between financial statement amounts are called

   a. Financial statement analysis
   b. Financial ratios
   c. Balance sheet comparisons
   d. Financial families

2. Which of the following ratios relates most closely to the concept of leverage?

   a. Current ratio
   b. Debt ratio
   c. PE ratio
   d. Asset turnover

3. Which of the following current ratios would be considered MOST liquid?

   a. 0.5
   b. 1.0
   c. 1.5
   d. 2.0

4. Return on sales

   a. measures the profitability of a company
   b. measures how many pennies of profit the company realizes for each dollar in sales
   c. must be evaluated in light of the appropriate industry
   d. All of the above

5. Asset turnover measures a company's

   a. efficiency
   b. liquidity
   c. profitability
   d. All of the above

6. The DuPont framework for computing return on equity includes each of the following components EXCEPT

   a. Return on sales
   b. Assets-to-equity ratio
   c. Debt ratio
   d. Asset turnover

7. Net income divided by stockholders' equity equals

    a. PE ratio
    b. Return on equity
    c. Return on sales
    d. Assets-to-equity ratio

8. Price-earnings ratio

    a. indicates the amount investors are willing to pay for each dollar of earnings
    b. is an indication of a company's growth potential
    c. is typically between 5 and 30 for most US companies
    d. All of the above

9. Dividing each financial statement number by sales results in

    a. Standardized financial statements
    b. Uniform financial statements
    c. Liquidated financial statements
    d. Common-size financial statements

10. Liquidity deals primarily with

    a. current assets and current liabilities
    b. revenues and expenses
    c. stockholders' equity
    d. long-term debt

11. The DuPont framework

    a. measures the liquidity of a company
    b. analyzes three components of return on equity
    c. was developed less than a decade ago
    d. All of the above

12. Cash flow ratios

    a. have been used less than 20 years
    b. are especially useful when a company has large noncash expenses
    c. are especially useful when a company experiences rapid growth
    d. All of the above

13. Cash flow from operations divided by net income equals

    a. Cash flow adequacy ratio
    b. Return on sales
    c. Cash flow-to-net income ratio
    d. Debt ratio

14. Financial statement analysis has the following potential pitfalls EXCEPT

    a. Financial statement numbers between companies and industries sometimes lack comparability.
    b. Few analysts actually perform any type of financial statement analysis.
    c. Financial statements do not contain all the information of a company.
    d. A struggling company's fatal flaw is not always revealed in the financial statements.

15. The examination of both the relationships among financial statement number and the trends in those numbers over time is called

    a. Financial statement analysis
    b. Financial statement investigation
    c. Forensic accounting
    d. Financial ratios

Exercises

E5-1 Computation of Ratios

Instructions: Using the following balance sheet and income statement information, compute the following ratios: (1) Debt ratio, (2) Current ratio, (3) Return on sales, (4) Asset turnover, (5) Return on equity, and (6) Price-earnings ratio.

Assets

Current assets:

Cash	$ 33,000
Accounts receivable	56,000
Total current assets	$ 89,000
Long-term investments	74,000
Property, plant, and equipment	165,000
Total assets	$ 328,000

Liabilities and stockholders' equity

Current liabilities:

Accounts payable	$ 47,000
Salaries payable	14,000
Total current liabilities	$ 61,000
Long-term liabilities	52,000
Total liabilities	$ 113,000
Stockholders' equity:	
Paid-in capital	$ 150,000
Retained earnings	65,000
Total stockholders' equity	$ 215,000
Total liabilities and stockholders' equity	$ 328,000

In addition, the following information for the year has been assembled:

Sales	$ 800,000
Net income	100,000
Market value at year-end	450,000

(1) Debt ratio

(2) Current ratio

(3) Return on sales

(4) Asset turnover

(5) Return on equity

(6) Price-earnings ratio

E5-2   Common-Size Income Statement

Instructions: Using the following information, prepare common-size income statements for the years 2006 and 2005.

	2006	2005
Sales	$400,000	$225,000
Cost of goods sold	(255,000)	(120,000)
Gross profit on sales	$145,000	$105,000
Selling and general expenses	(50,000)	(40,000)
Operating income	$95,000	$65,000
Interest expense	(20,000)	(15,000)
Income before income tax	$75,000	$50,000
Income tax expense	(22,500)	(15,000)
Net income	$52,500	$35,000

_____
_____
_____
_____
_____
_____
_____
_____
_____
_____
_____
_____
_____
_____
_____

E5-3   Common-Size Balance Sheet

Instructions: Using the following information, prepare a common-size balance sheet for the year. Sales for the year was $750,000.

Assets
Current assets:

Cash	$ 33,000
Accounts receivable	56,000
Total current assets	$ 89,000
Long-term investments	74,000
Property, plant, and equipment	165,000
Total assets	$ 328,000

Liabilities and stockholders' equity
Current liabilities:

Accounts payable	$ 47,000
Salaries payable	14,000
Total current liabilities	$ 61,000
Long-term liabilities	52,000
Total liabilities	$ 113,000
Stockholders' equity:	
Paid-in capital	$ 150,000
Retained earnings	65,000
Total stockholders' equity	$ 215,000
Total liabilities and stockholders' equity	$ 328,000

_____
_____
_____
_____
_____
_____
_____
_____
_____
_____
_____
_____
_____
_____
_____
_____
_____
_____
_____
_____
_____
_____
_____
_____
_____
_____
_____
_____

E5-4   DuPont Framework

Instructions: Using the following information, compute (1) Return on equity, (2) Return on sales, (3) Asset turnover, and (4) Assets-to-equity ratio for 2006, 2005 and 2004.

	2006	2005	2004
Current assets	$ 60,000	$ 50,000	$ 70,000
Total assets	200,000	160,000	180,000
Current liabilities	40,000	30,000	30,000
Total liabilities	90,000	80,000	100,000
Stockholders' equity	110,000	80,000	80,000
Sales	800,000	600,000	600,000
Net income	40,000	20,000	10,000

(1) Return on equity

(2) Return on sales

(3) Asset turnover

(4) Assets-to-equity ratio

ANSWERS

Matching

1.	k	5.	e	9.	a
2.	d	6.	j	10.	c
3.	b	7.	f	11.	i
4.	l	8.	h	12.	g

True/False

1.	T	6.	F	11.	T
2.	F	7.	T	12.	F
3.	T	8.	T	13.	T
4.	T	9.	T	14.	T
5.	F	10.	F	15.	F

Multiple Choice

1.	b	6.	c	11.	b
2.	b	7.	b	12.	d
3.	d	8.	d	13.	c
4.	d	9.	d	14.	b
5.	a	10.	a	15.	a

Exercises

E5-1   Computation of Ratios

(1) Debt ratio $=$ $\dfrac{\text{Total liabilities}}{\text{Total assets}}$ $=$ $\dfrac{\$113,000}{\$328,000}$ $=$ 34.45%

(2) Current ratio $=$ $\dfrac{\text{Current assets}}{\text{Current liabilities}}$ $=$ $\dfrac{\$89,000}{\$61,000}$ $=$ 1.46

(3) Return on sales $=$ $\dfrac{\text{Net income}}{\text{Sales}}$ $=$ $\dfrac{\$100,000}{\$800,000}$ $=$ 12.5%

(4) Asset turnover $=$ $\dfrac{\text{Sales}}{\text{Total assets}}$ $=$ $\dfrac{\$800,000}{\$328,000}$ $=$ 2.44

(5) Return on equity $=$ $\dfrac{\text{Net income}}{\text{Total stockholders' equity}}$ $=$ $\dfrac{\$100,000}{\$215,000}$ $=$ 46.5%

(6) Price-earnings ratio $=$ $\dfrac{\text{Market value of shares}}{\text{Net income}}$ $=$ $\dfrac{\$450,000}{\$100,000}$ $=$ 4.50

E5-2   Common-Size Income Statement

	2006	%	2005	%
Sales	$400,000	100.0%	$225,000	100.0%
Cost of goods sold	(255,000)	63.8%	(120,000)	53.3%
Gross profit on sales	$145,000	36.3%	$105,000	46.7%
Selling and general expenses	(50,000)	12.5%	(40,000)	17.8%
Operating income	$95,000	23.8%	$65,000	28.9%
Interest expense	(20,000)	5.0%	(15,000)	6.7%
Income before income tax	$75,000	18.8%	$50,000	22.2%
Income tax expense	(22,500)	5.6%	(15,000)	6.7%
Net income	$52,500	13.1%	$35,000	15.6%

E5-3   Common-Size Balance Sheet

Assets
Current assets:

Cash	$ 33,000	4.4%
Accounts receivable	56,000	7.5%
Total current assets	$ 89,000	11.9%
Long-term investments	74,000	9.9%
Property, plant, and equipment	165,000	22.0%
Total assets	$ 328,000	43.7%

Liabilities and stockholders' equity
Current liabilities:

Accounts payable	$ 47,000	6.3%
Salaries payable	14,000	1.9%
Total current liabilities	$ 61,000	8.1%
Long-term liabilities	52,000	6.9%
Total liabilities	$ 113,000	15.1%

Stockholders' equity:

Paid-in capital	$ 150,000	20.0%
Retained earnings	65,000	8.7%
Total stockholders' equity	$ 215,000	28.7%
Total liabilities and stockholders' equity	$ 328,000	43.7%

E5-4   DuPont Framework

	2006	2005	2004
(1) Return on equity	36.4%	25.0%	12.5%
(2) Return on sales	5.0%	3.3%	1.7%
(3) Asset turnover	4.00	3.75	3.33
(4) Assets-to-equity ratio	1.82	2.00	2.25

Chapter 6
Ensuring the Integrity of Financial Information

LEARNING OBJECTIVES

After studying this chapter, you should be able to:

1. Identify the types of problems that can make their way into financial statements.

2. Describe the safeguards employed within a firm to ensure that financial statements are free from problems.

3. Understand the concept of earnings management and why it occurs.

4. Understand the major parts of the Sarbanes-Oxley Act and how it impacts financial reporting.

5. Describe the role of auditors and how their presence affects the integrity of financial statements.

6. Explain the role of the Securities and Exchange Commission in adding credibility to financial statements.

CHAPTER REVIEW

The Types of Problems that Can Occur

1. Financial statements are usually prepared with integrity and are accurate. However, both unintentional errors and intentional deception can result in financial statements that contain errors and are misleading.

2. Errors can occur in most stages of the accounting cycle. Most often, however, errors and fraud occur at the transaction stage of the cycle. These errors usually flow forward to make the financial statements misleading.

3. Errors that occur at the posting or ledger stage of the accounting cycle usually involve (1) not summarizing journal entry data appropriately or (2) posting amounts to incorrect accounts.

4. Accounting involves making many judgments. Errors or disagreements in judgment can cause financial statements to be incorrect.

5. Fraud can also cause financial statements to be incorrect. Financial statement fraud occurs when managers intentionally manipulate the financial statements to serve their own purposes.

Safeguards Designed to Minimize Problems

6. The four major safeguards built into the financial reporting process in the United States are (1) the internal control structure, (2) internal auditors, (3) external auditors, and (4) the Securities and

Exchange Commission. These safeguards protect investors and creditors who rely on financial statements and help management to know their financial reporting is sound.

7. The internal control structure refers to the safeguards organizations who prepare financial statements build into their financial reporting and accounting processes. Internal control structures have five purposes: (1) to provide reliable data in financial reports, (2) to safeguard assets and records, (3) to help provide for the efficiency and effectiveness of operations, (4) to ensure that management policies are followed, and (5) to ensure compliance with the Foreign Corrupt Practices Act.

8. The Foreign Corrupt Practices Act was a law passed by Congress in 1977 that requires publicly traded companies to keep records and have controls in place to ensure that transactions are recorded accurately and fairly.

9. The Sarbanes-Oxley Act was a law passed by Congress in 2002 that requires a number of changes in financial reporting, including an "internal control report" and management certification of the "appropriateness of the financial statements and disclosures contained in the report."

10. The internal control structures of most corporations have three elements: (1) the control environment, (2) the accounting system, and (3) control activities.

The Control Environment

11. The control environment of most organizations includes (1) management's philosophy and operating style, (2) organizational structure, and (3) an audit committee, among other things. It is important that a proper control environment be established so that employees and others are taught appropriate behavior and can see the appropriate modeling of behavior.

The Accounting System

12. In order to provide safeguards to financial reporting, accounting systems should include processes and characteristics that ensure (1) only valid transactions are recorded, (2) only properly authorized transactions are recorded, (3) recorded transactions are complete, (4) transactions are properly classified, (5) transactions are recorded on a timely basis and in the correct periods, (6)

transactions are properly valued, and (7) transactions are correctly posted and summarized.

Control Procedures

13. The five major control procedures (activities) most organizations have in place are (1) adequate segregation of duties, (2) procedures for authorization, (3) adequate documents and records, (4) physical control over assets and records, and (5) independent checks on performance.

14. It is a requirement that public companies include in their annual report a statement about their internal controls acknowledging that it is the company's responsibility to have a good system of internal controls.

Earnings Management

15. A number of reasons exist for why management would want to manage its earnings. Some of these reasons are (1) to meet internal targets, (2) to meet external expectations, (3) to smooth increases in income over time, and (4) to make the company more attractive for an IPO or a loan.

16. Companies can manage earnings across a long continuum. The points on the earnings management continuum are (1) strategic matching of transactions, (2) changes in methods or estimates with full disclosure, (3) changes in methods or estimates but with little or no disclosure, (4) non-GAAP accounting, and (5) fictitious transactions.

17. Everyone agrees that creating fictitious transactions is unethical, but debates arise along the other points of the earnings management continuum. Personal ethics are closely connected with financial accounting and should be used when preparing and auditing financial statements.

The Sarbanes-Oxley Act

18. The three major effects of the creation of the Sarbanes-Oxley Act are (1) the establishment of independent oversight of auditors, (2) additional constraints on auditors, and (3) additional constraints on company management.

The Role of Auditors in the Accounting Process

19. Two types of auditors are discussed in the chapter: internal auditors and external auditors. Internal auditors are independent control experts who work for firms producing the financial statements. Their job includes independently evaluating con-

trols over financial reporting, detecting fraud in their organization, and helping to ensure that operations are effective and efficient. Internal auditors usually report directly to an organization's board of directors so they are "independent" of management.

20. External auditors are independent professionals who examine the financial statements of organizations and render audit opinions on those financial statements. External auditors attest to the level that their clients' financial statements follow generally accepted accounting principles (GAAP).

21. Independent audits are usually performed by certified public accountants (CPAs) who have passed the rigorous certified public accountancy examination administered by the American Institute of Certified Public Accountants. CPAs must perform their audits by following generally accepted auditing standards (GAAS).

22. Auditors use various types of evidence gathering procedures when performing audits. They observe what is going on, they examine documents and records, and they make inquiries of people, both within and outside the company.

23. While audits cannot "guarantee" accuracy in financial statements, they do add credibility.

The Securities and Exchange Commission

24. The Securities and Exchange Commission (SEC) is a governmental agency whose purpose is to help ensure that information provided to investors is accurate and fair and to regulate trading of financial markets.

25. Public companies whose stock is traded on stock markets must file several reports with the SEC. Registration statements must be filed when a company wants to issue stock or debt to the public. Form 10-K is the annual report that must be filed with the SEC. Form 10-Q is the quarterly report that must be filed with the SEC. SEC forms generally require the inclusion of financial statements that are audited or reviewed by independent CPAs.

26. The SEC is a powerful organization that can sanction CPAs, suspend trading of a company's stock, establish accounting standards for public companies, and stop companies from raising money through the selling of stocks or bonds.

COMMON ERRORS

This chapter is conceptual rather than problem oriented. There are no parts that are especially difficult or errors that are commonly made in this chapter. It is important to realize that both internal controls and internal auditors are safeguards of the companies preparing financial reports. External auditors are independent CPAs who review the company's financial statements. The responsibility of external auditors is to protect the public, even though they are paid by the client. Companies are required by the SEC, a governmental agency, to have their financial statements audited by CPAs.

SELF-TEST

Matching

Instructions: Write the letter of each of the following terms in the space to the left of its appropriate definition.

a.	Securities and Exchange Commission	f.	Form 10-K
b.	audit committee	g.	Form 10-Q
c.	control environment	h.	internal control structure
d.	control procedures	i.	external auditors
e.	earnings management	j.	Sarbanes-Oxley Act

_____   1. Policies and procedures used by management to meet its objectives and ensure its financial reports are accurate; generally divided into five categories; sometimes called control activities.

_____   2. Actions, policies, and procedures that reflect the overall attitudes of top management, the directors, and the owners about control and its importance to the organization.

_____   3. Comprised of outside directors to whom internal and external auditors report.

_____   4. Annual report filed with the SEC.

_____   5. An agency of the Federal government.

_____   6. Safeguards in the form of policies and procedures established to provide management with reasonable assurance that the objectives of an organization will be achieved.

_____   7. Quarterly report filed with the SEC.

_____   8. CPAs that review a company's financial statements to see if they are prepared and presented in accordance with generally accepted accounting principles.

_____   9. The process of using accounting rules to manipulate earnings to meet internal targets or external expectations.

_____ 10. Legislation passed in 2002 that greatly affected audits of public companies.

True/False

Instructions: Place a check mark in the appropriate column to indicate whether each of the following statements is true or false.

	True	False
1. Organizational structure is an element of the control procedures.		
2. Segregation of duties is an element of the control environment.		
3. Independent checks on performance is an element of the control procedures.		
4. External auditors provide a monitoring role for financial statements.		
5. The SEC is a private organization similar to the FASB.		
6. The Foreign Corrupt Practices Act requires companies to maintain good internal controls.		
7. Errors in judgment can cause financial statements to be wrong.		
8. Having a good organizational structure is a control procedure.		
9. Form 10-Q is the annual report that must be filed with the SEC by public companies.		
10. CPAs must perform their audits in conformance with GAAP.		
11. Validity is a control objective of an accounting system.		
12. Having adequate documents and records is part of the control environment.		
13. External auditors receive their audit fees from the SEC.		

	True	False
14. GAAS and GAAP are the same thing.	_____	_____
15. A company generally would issue more than one Form 10-Q per year.	_____	_____
16. The SEC has the power to suspend trading of a company's stock.	_____	_____
17. Most people agree that creation of fictitious transactions is ethical.	_____	_____
18. The Sarbanes-Oxley Act required the establishment of the Public Company Accounting Oversight Board.	_____	_____

Multiple Choice

Instructions: Circle the letter that best completes each of the following statements.

1. Which of the following is *not* a type of internal control procedure?

    a. Segregation of duties
    b. Proper authorizations
    c. Independent checks
    d. Audit committee

2. Which of the following is *not* an element of a good accounting system?

    a. Proper classification
    b. Proper timing
    c. Proper valuation
    d. Physical control

3. Which of the following is *not* associated with external auditors?

    a. Being paid by the client
    b. CPA examination
    c. Must follow GAAS
    d. Work for the company they audit

4. Which of the following organizations is a government entity?

    a. AICPA
    b. IIA
    c. SEC
    d. FASB

5. Which of the following is *not* a type of evidence gathering technique used by independent CPAs?

    a. Interviews
    b. Subpoenas
    c. Examination of documents
    d. Observations

6. Which of the following is *not* an organization or group that monitors controls or financial statements?

    a. SEC
    b. External auditor
    c. Internal Revenue Service
    d. Internal auditor

7. Recording fictitious sales would result in all of the following *except*

    a. overstating net income.
    b. overstating revenues.
    c. overstating inventory.
    d. overstating accounts receivable.

8. Who is responsible for issuing the report on internal controls that accompanies a company's financial statements?

    a. External auditors
    b. Management
    c. SEC
    d. IRS

9. Which of the following groups can suspend the trading of a company's stock?

    a. SEC
    b. Internal auditing profession
    c. External auditors
    d. CPAs

10. Which of the following is *not* a purpose of the internal control structure?

    a. Ensuring that accounting reports provide reliable data
    b. Aiding the effectiveness and efficiency of operations
    c. Ensuring compliance with the Foreign Corrupt Practices Act
    d. Ensuring that fraud never occurs in the organization

11. The organizational structure of a firm is considered to be part of its

    a. control environment.
    b. control procedures.
    c. accounting system.
    d. monitoring activities.

12. Having different individuals perform authorization, recordkeeping, and custodial activities is known as

    a. proper authorization.
    b. segregation of duties.
    c. physical safeguards.
    d. independent checks.

13. Internal auditors generally work for the

    a. company producing the financial statements.
    b. CPA firm.
    c. SEC.
    d. AICPA.

14. The standards by which external audits must be conducted are referred to as

    a. GAAP.
    b. GAAS.
    c. SEC.
    d. FCPA.

15. Errors can occur in the financial statements from

    a. mistakes in judgment.
    b. fraud.
    c. unintentional errors.
    d. All of the above

16. The best way to describe independent audits is that they

    a. guarantee accuracy of financial statements.
    b. add credibility to financial statements.
    c. are required of all companies.
    d. are performed by internal auditors.

17. Earnings management techniques include

    a. strategic matching of transactions
    b. changes in methods or estimates with full disclosure
    c. fictitious transactions
    d. All of the above

18. The Sarbanes-Oxley Act created all of the following EXCEPT

    a. the establishment of an independent oversight board
    b. the abolishment of the FASB
    c. additional constraints on auditors
    d. additional constraints on company management

Exercises

Because of the conceptual nature of this chapter, there are no exercises.

ANSWERS

Matching

1.	d	6.	h	
2.	c	7.	g	
3.	b	8.	i	
4.	f	9.	e	
5.	a	10.	j	

True/False

1.	F	7.	T	13.	F
2.	F	8.	F	14.	F
3.	T	9.	F	15.	T
4.	T	10.	F	16.	T
5.	F	11.	T	17.	F
6.	T	12.	F	18.	T

Multiple Choice

1.	d	7.	c	13.	a
2.	d	8.	b	14.	b
3.	d	9.	a	15.	d
4.	c	10.	d	16.	b
5.	b	11.	a	17.	d
6.	c	12.	b	18.	b

Chapter 7
Selling a Product or Service

LEARNING OBJECTIVES

After studying this chapter, you should be able to:

1. Understand the three basic types of business activities: operating, investing, and financing.

2. Use the two revenue recognition criteria to decide when the revenue from a sale or service should be recorded in the accounting records.

3. Properly account for the collection of cash and describe the business controls necessary to safeguard cash.

4. Record the losses resulting from credit customers who do not pay their bills.

5. Evaluate a company's management of its receivables by computing and analyzing appropriate financial ratios.

6. Match revenues and expenses by estimating and recording future warranty and service costs associated with a sale.

EXPANDED MATERIAL LEARNING OBJECTIVES

7. Reconcile a checking account.

8. Account for the impact of changing exchange rates on the value of accounts receivable denominated in foreign currencies.

CHAPTER REVIEW

Major Activities of a Business

1. Activities of a business can be divided into three groups: (1) operating activities, (2) investing activities, and (3) financing activities.

2. Operating activities involve selling products and/or services, buying inventory for resale, and incurring and paying for necessary expenses associated with the primary activities of the business.

3. Investing activities involve purchasing assets for use in the business. Operating assets purchased include such items as property, plant, and equipment. Nonoperating assets purchased include such items as investments in stocks and bonds of other companies.

4. Financing activities involve raising money by means other than operations to finance a business. Financing activities include borrowing money and selling stock.

Recognizing Revenue

5. Revenues are increases in resources from the sale of goods or the performance of services. Revenues are usually recognized when (1) the work has been substantially completed, and (2) cash, or a valid promise of future payment, has been received.

6. In most cases, revenues are recognized when goods are shipped to customers.

7. When there is significant uncertainty about whether cash from a sale will be collected, revenue should probably be recognized when cash is collected.

8. When sales are made in advance, such as with airline tickets or athletic season tickets, revenues are usually recognized when the service is performed (flight is taken or game is attended).

Cash Collection

9. Sales discounts, or cash discounts, are reductions in the amount customers owe if payment is made within a specified time limit. A typical discount is 2/10, n/30, which means that customers receive a 2 percent discount if payment is made within 10 days of the date of purchase, and the total amount is due within 30 days.

10. Typical entries needed to account for sales, receivables, and sales discounts are shown below, when 1/10, n/30 sales terms are given on a $1,000 sale.

Transaction	Journal Entries		
Sale	Accounts Receivable	1,000	
	Sales Revenue		1,000
Payment (if made within the discount period)	Cash..........................	990	
	Sales Discounts	10	
	Accounts Receivable		1,000
Payment (if not made within the discount period)	Cash..........................	1,000	
	Accounts Receivable		1,000

11. When merchandise previously sold is returned, an account called Sales Returns and Allowances is debited and either Accounts Receivable or Cash is credited.

12. Both Sales Discounts and Sales Returns and Allowances are contra-revenue accounts that are deducted from gross sales revenue on the income statement.

13. Because cash is so liquid, companies usually develop elaborate internal control systems to protect it. Common internal controls for cash are:

   a. Separation of the duties in accounting for and handling of cash. (This helps prevent the practice of *lapping* by employees.)
   b. The daily depositing of all cash receipts in bank accounts.
   c. The use of prenumbered checks to make all cash disbursements.

Accounting for Credit Customers Who Don't Pay

14. Receivables are a company's claims for money, goods, or services. Receivables arise when merchandise is sold or services are performed on credit.

15. Accounts receivable are short-term liquid assets that arise from credit sales to customers. When companies sell goods or services on credit, the entry includes a debit to Accounts Receivable and a credit to Sales Revenue. When the receivable is collected, Cash is debited and Accounts Receivable is credited.

16. When customers do not pay the amount they owe, bad-debt losses occur.

17. There are two well-known methods of accounting for uncollectible receivables. The direct write-off method recognizes a loss from a receivable at the time it is deemed to be uncollectible. Since uncollectibility is often determined several months after a sale takes place, this method sometimes violates the matching principle, and thus is not allowed under generally accepted accounting principles. The allowance method satisfies the matching principle by requiring that estimates of uncollectible receivables be made in the same period that sales are recognized. The journal entry recording the estimate is usually made as an adjusting entry at the end of the accounting period.

18. The most common methods of estimating the amount of uncollectible accounts receivable when using the allowance method are (1) a straight percentage of credit sales, (2) a percentage of receivables, and (3) aging the accounts receivables.

19. When estimating bad debt expense as a percentage of credit sales, the existing balance in Allowance for Bad Debts, if there is one, is not considered in the adjusting entry.

20. "Aging" receivables refers to the process whereby receivables are classified according to age, such as current, 1–30 days past due, 31–60 days past due, and so on. Then an estimate is made of the amount of uncollectible receivables in each category.

Assessing How Well Companies Manage Their Receivables

21. Organizations use two ratios to evaluate how well they manage their resources: (1) accounts receivable turnover and (2) average collection period. Accounts receivable turnover is calculated by dividing total sales for the period by accounts receivable. Average collection period is calculated by dividing 365 (days in a year) by the accounts receivable turnover ratio.

Recording Warranty and Service Costs Associated With a Sale

22. Organizations that provide warranties on the products or services they sell must recognize those customer service expenses in the period in which the sale takes place. A proper matching requires that an estimate be made of future warranty expenses related to the current period's sales.

23. When accounting for warranties, the entry to record the estimate of future expenditures includes a debit to Customer Service Expense and a credit to Estimated Liability for Service. When services are performed, Estimated Liability for Service is debited and Wages Payable and Supplies are credited.

EXPANDED MATERIAL

Reconciling the Bank Account

24. The ending cash balance shown on the bank statement usually will not agree with the cash balance reported on the company's books. It is important that this difference be accounted for and that the accounting records be adjusted to bring the accounts to the correct balances. The most common reasons for differences between the bank statement and the company's books are:

   a. Time-period differences.
   b. Deposits in transit.
   c. Outstanding checks.
   d. Bank debits not reflected in the books.
   e. Bank credits not reflected in the books.
   f. Errors made either by the bank or by the company.

25. The format for a bank reconciliation follows. (*Note:* Errors may be added to or deducted from either side, depending on whether the bank or the company made the error.)

Balance per bank	xxx	Balance per books	xxx
Add deposits in transit	xx	Add credits by bank	xx
Deduct outstanding checks	(xx)	Deduct debits by bank	(xx)
Corrected cash balance	xxx	Corrected cash balance	xxx

All adjustments to the book balance require journal entries that either debit or credit Cash. Adjustments to the bank balance do not require any entries in the company's books.

Understand How Changing Exchange Rates Affect the Valuation of Accounts Receivable

26. A foreign currency transaction is a transaction that is denominated in a currency other than the company's typical currency.

27. When a company has a foreign currency transaction, gains or losses from exchange rate changes are accounted for in the period in which those exchange rates change. With this adjustment, the balance sheet will reflect the transaction value as of the balance sheet.

COMMON ERRORS

The two most common errors made when studying this chapter are:

1. Confusing the percentage of sales and percentage of receivables methods for estimating uncollectible accounts receivable.

2. Incorrectly calculating gains or losses on foreign currency exchanges.

---

1. **Estimation Methods of Uncollectible Receivables**

   Most students quickly understand why the allowance method of accounting for losses from uncollectible receivables is preferred over the direct write-off method. You can see that the direct write-off method often violates the important matching principle, especially for sales made near the end of an accounting period.

   The same distinction can be made between the percentage of sales and the percentage of receivables estimation methods. The former enforces the matching principle, and the latter violates it. Sales are reported on the income statement, which includes transactions from only one period, since income statement accounts are closed every year. Accounts Receivable is a balance sheet account and, strictly speaking, the balance in receivables could come from any period. In the first case, where the estimate is a percentage of sales, the matching principle is enforced and any existing balance in the allowance account, which relates to prior periods, is ignored. With the percentage of receivables method, the existing balance in Allowance for Bad Debts must be considered because receivables could come from any period. To reinforce this idea, consider the following example:

Account Balance at 12/31/03 (Before Adjustment)

Accounts Receivable	$100,000
Allowance for Bad Debts	350 (credit balance)
Sales Revenue	220,000

Under the percentage of sales method, the $350 is assumed to be left from the previous year. If 1 percent of sales are considered uncollectible in the current year, $2,200 (0.01 × $220,000) would be added to the Allowance account and the balance would be $2,550 ($2,200 + $350).

Under the percentage of receivables method, the $350 is assumed to be associated with the receivables (which could come from any period). If 2 percent of receivables are considered uncollectible, only $1,650 [(100,000 × 0.02) − $350] would be added to the account.

2. **Determining a Gain or Loss on Changes in Exchange Rates**

Foreign currencies can go up or down in value and result in a gain or loss depending on whether the transaction resulted in a receivable or a payable. That is, changes in exchange rates will have a different effect depending on whether the goods were bought or sold.

For example, if exchange rates increase, then a company will pay more (in the case of an accounts payable) or receive more (in the case of an accounts receivable). The reverse is true if exchange rates decrease.

For example, suppose a U.S. company purchases inventory from a French company for 1,000,000 French francs when the French franc is valued at $0.07. If payment is made on the day of the sale, the U.S. company would pay the equivalent of $70,000 (1,000,000 francs × $0.07). If the amount is not due for 30 days, then the U.S. company would record a payable in the amount of $70,000. The amount to be paid in 30 days would depend on the exchange rate on the date of payment. If the exchange rate had changed to one French franc being worth $0.09, then the U.S. company would be required to pay $90,000 (1,000,000 × $0.09) to purchase 1,000,000 French francs resulting in a loss to the U.S. company of $20,000 (1,000,000 francs × $0.02).

If the U.S. company had been the seller instead of the buyer in the previous example, then the company would have recorded a gain upon receipt of the 1,000,000 French francs as they would be worth $90,000 instead of the $70,000 that would have been originally recorded on the date of the sale.

SELF-TEST
Matching

Instructions: Write the letter of each of the following terms in the space to the left of its appropriate definition.

a.	receivable		**g.**	accounts receivable turnover
b.	allowance method		**h.**	average collection period
c.	account receivable		**i.**	net realizable value
d.	sales discount		**j.**	revenue recognition
e.	allowance for bad debts		**k.**	investing activities
f.	direct write-off method		**l.**	foreign currency transaction

_____ 1. A reduction in the sales price that is allowed if payment is received within a specified period; also called cash discount.

_____ 2. Claims for money, goods, or services.

_____ 3. The recording of estimated losses due to uncollectible accounts as expenses during the period in which the sales occurred.

_____ 4. Sales divided by accounts receivable.

_____ 5. A contra-account, deducted from Accounts Receivable, that shows the estimated losses from uncollectible accounts.

_____ 6. Money due from rendering services or selling merchandise on credit.

_____ 7. 365 divided by accounts receivable turnover.

_____ 8. The recording of actual losses from uncollectible accounts as expenses during the period in which accounts receivable are determined to be uncollectible.

_____ 9. The net amount of accounts receivable; equal to accounts receivable less allowance for bad debts.

_____ 10. Recording of a sale through a journal entry.

_____ 11. Purchasing assets for use in the business.

EXPANDED MATERIAL

_____ 12. A transaction that is denominated in a foreign currency.

True/False

Instructions: Place a check mark in the appropriate column to indicate whether each of the following statements is true or false.

	True	False
1. The main criterion for deciding whether or not to recognize a revenue is usually cash collection.	_____	_____
2. Accounts receivable arise when merchandise is purchased from suppliers.	_____	_____
3. A 2/10, n/30 sales discount means that 10 percent interest will be charged if the account is not paid within 30 days.	_____	_____
4. When recording credit sales, Accounts Receivable is debited.	_____	_____
5. The Sales Discounts and Sales Returns and Allowances accounts are contra-revenue accounts.	_____	_____
6. Accounts receivable are usually *not* interest-bearing.	_____	_____
7. When collecting credit sales, Accounts Receivable is debited.	_____	_____
8. The direct write-off method of accounting for uncollectible receivables is required under generally accepted accounting principles.	_____	_____
9. The allowance method of accounting for uncollectible receivables is an estimation method.	_____	_____

	True	False
10. An aging of accounts receivable identifies which customers are most delinquent in their payments.	_____	_____
11. Warranty expenses are always recognized in the period when incurred or paid.	_____	_____
12. Accounts receivable turnover is calculated by dividing 365 by credit sales for the period.	_____	_____

EXPANDED MATERIAL

13. Interest earned on a bank account is subtracted from the "balance per books" on a bank reconciliation.	_____	_____
14. If a U.S. company has a receivable denominated in a foreign currency and exchange rates increase, the company will record a gain.	_____	_____
15. If a U.S. company has a payable denominated in a foreign currency and exchange rates increase, the company will record a loss.	_____	_____

Multiple Choice

Instructions: Circle the letter that best completes each of the following statements.

1. Buying inventory for resale is considered to be a(n)

    a. operating activity.
    b. investing activity.
    c. financing activity.
    d. operating asset.

2. Revenues are

    a. reported on the balance sheet.
    b. reported on the statement of cash flows.
    c. reported on the income statement.
    d. liabilities.

3. Net sales (in a merchandising firm) is equal to

    a. gross sales minus sales discounts plus sales returns and allowances.
    b. gross sales minus sales discounts minus sales returns and allowances.
    c. gross sales plus sales discounts plus sales returns and allowances.
    d. gross sales.

4. When merchandise is sold on credit

    a. Sales Revenue is debited.
    b. Cash is debited.
    c. Accounts Receivable is debited.
    d. Accounts Receivable is credited.

5. A sales discount of 2/10, n/30 means that

    a. a 2 percent discount will be allowed if payment is received within 30 days.
    b. the net amount must be paid within 10 days.
    c. interest of 10 percent will be charged after 30 days.
    d. a 2 percent discount will be allowed if payment is made within 10 days, but the full amount must be paid in 30 days.

6. The Sales Returns and Allowances account is a(n)

    a. revenue account.
    b. contra-revenue account.
    c. liability account.
    d. asset account.

7. The direct write-off method of accounting for uncollectible receivables usually

    a. violates the matching principle.
    b. is an estimation method.
    c. is allowed under generally accepted accounting principles.
    d. violates the going concern assumption.

8. The allowance method of accounting for uncollectible receivables

    a. is an estimation method.
    b. violates the matching principle.
    c. Both *a* and *b*
    d. violates GAAP.

9. An aging of accounts receivable

    a. helps identify slow-paying customers.
    b. is a method of estimating uncollectible receivables.
    c. Both *a* and *b*
    d. None of the above

10. ABC Company has a credit balance of $200 in Allowance for Bad Debts. If it estimates that 2 percent of this year's total sales of $45,000 are uncollectible, Bad Debt Expense would be

    a. debited for $900.
    b. credited for $900.
    c. debited for $700.
    d. credited for $700.

11. The net realizable value of receivables is equal to

    a. total accounts receivable plus the allowance for bad debts.
    b. total accounts receivable less the allowance for bad debts.
    c. total accounts receivable only.
    d. total accounts receivable plus cash.

12. The denominator in the "average collection period" calculation is

    a. 365.
    b. accounts receivable turnover.
    c. average receivables.
    d. credit sales.

13. Warranty (Customer Service) liabilities are recorded

    a. in the same period as the products are sold.
    b. in periods subsequent to the sale.
    c. in periods prior to the sale.
    d. only when cash is paid to provide customer service.

EXPANDED MATERIAL

14. NSF checks are included on a bank reconciliation as a(n)

    a. addition to the "balance per bank."
    b. deduction from the "balance per bank."
    c. addition to the "balance per books."
    d. deduction from the "balance per books."

15. A U.S. company sold inventory to a Japanese company for 5,000,000 yen due in 30 days. On the date of the transaction, one Japanese yen is worth $0.02. When the receivable is collected, the exchange rate is $0.03. On the date of collection, the U.S. company would record

    a. an exchange gain of $50,000.
    b. an exchange loss of $50,000.
    c. an increase in the receivable of $50,000.
    d. a decrease in the receivable of $50,000.

Exercises

E7-1   Sales Entries

Maxey Company is a wholesale clothing distributor that sells women's coats to clothing stores. During January the firm had the following transactions.

Jan.   3   Sold 8 coats that cost $120 each on account to Paris Clothing Store at $200 each (terms 2/10, n/30).
    5   Sold 5 coats that cost $100 each on account to Extravaganza Clothing Store at $200 each (terms 2/10, n/30).
  11   Received payment in full from Paris Clothing Store.
  19   Received payment in full from Extravaganza Clothing Store.

Instructions: Provide journal entries to account for these transactions.

JOURNAL   PAGE

DATE	DESCRIPTION	POST. REF.	DEBIT	CREDIT

E7-2   Accounting for Accounts Receivable

During 2006, Johnson Manufacturing had sales of $2,000,000, 70 percent of which were on credit. Also during 2006, $20,000 of accounts receivable were written off as uncollectible. At December 31, 2006, the Accounts Receivable balance showed a total of $300,000, which was aged as follows:

Age	Amount
Current	$200,000
1–30 days past due	70,000
31–60 days past due	20,000
61–90 days past due	8,000
Over 90 days past due	2,000
Total	$300,000

Instructions: Prepare the journal entries required on December 31, 2006, to properly record the bad debt expense under each of the following methods. (Assume, where applicable, that the credit balance in Allowance for Bad Debts is $3,000 before any adjusting entries at December 31, 2006.)

1. The direct write-off method. (Assume that all accounts determined to be uncollectible are written off in a single year-end entry.)
2. Based on experience, uncollectible accounts for the year are estimated to be approximately 4 percent of the Accounts Receivable balance.
3. Based on experience, uncollectible accounts are estimated to be the sum of:
   - 0.5% of current accounts
   - 1.5% of accounts 1–30 days past due
   - 3.0% of accounts 31–60 days past due
   - 10.0% of accounts 61–90 days past due
   - 30.0% of accounts 90 days past due

JOURNAL   PAGE

DATE	DESCRIPTION	POST. REF.	DEBIT	CREDIT

E7-3   Accounting for Accounts Receivable

Assume the same data as in E7-2. Also assume that based on experience, uncollectible accounts are estimated to be approximately 1 percent of total credit sales for the year.

Instructions: Make the journal entry as of December 31, 2006, to record the bad debts expense.

JOURNAL   **PAGE**

DATE	DESCRIPTION	POST. REF.	DEBIT	CREDIT

E7-4   Assessing How Well Companies Manage Their Receivables

Tanner Company has the following data related to its sales and receivables:

Total Credit Sales—2005	$2,000,000
Total Credit Sales—2006	2,500,000
Accounts Receivable Balances:	
January 1, 2005	180,000
December 31, 2005	300,000
December 31, 2006	500,000

Instructions: Based on these numbers, calculate the following:

1. Accounts receivable turnover for 2005.
2. Accounts receivable turnover for 2006.
3. Average collection period for 2005.
4. Average collection period for 2006.

E7-5   Accounting for Warranty Expense

RTV sells stereo systems with a 2-year warranty. Past experience indicates that 10 percent of all systems sold will require repairs during the first year and an additional 20 percent will need repairs during the second year. The average cost to repair a system is $50. The number of systems sold in 2005 and 2006 was 5,000 and 6,000, respectively. Actual repair costs were $12,500 in 2005 and $55,000 in 2006.

Instructions: Assume all repair costs involve cash expenditures and provide journal entries to account for the following:

1. 2005 actual customer service costs.
2. Estimated warranty expense at 12/31/02 to account for warranty work that will be done in the future related to 2005 sales.
3. 2006 actual customer service costs.
4. Estimated warranty expense at 12/31/2006 to account for warranty that will be done in the future related to 2006 sales.

JOURNAL   PAGE

DATE	DESCRIPTION	POST. REF.	DEBIT	CREDIT

E7-6   (Expanded material) Foreign Currency Transactions

On June 1, ABC Company purchased inventory from Canadian Company agreeing to pay 100,000 Canadian dollars on July 1. On June 1, the exchange is $0.75 per U.S. dollar, and on July 1 the exchange rate is $0.77 per U.S. dollar. On July 1, ABC Company paid 100,000 Canadian dollars to Canadian Company.

Instructions: Provide the necessary entries to account for the June 1 and July 1 transactions for ABC Company.

JOURNAL   PAGE

DATE		DESCRIPTION	POST. REF.	DEBIT	CREDIT

ANSWERS

Matching

1.	d	5.	e	9.	i
2.	a	6.	c	10.	j
3.	b	7.	h	11.	k
4.	g	8.	f	12.	l

True/False

1.	F	6.	T	11.	F
2.	F	7.	F	12.	F
3.	F	8.	F	13.	F
4.	T	9.	T	14.	T
5.	T	10.	T	15.	T

Multiple Choice

1.	a	6.	b	11.	b
2.	c	7.	a	12.	b
3.	b	8.	a	13.	a
4.	c	9.	c	14.	d
5.	d	10.	a	15.	a

Exercises

E7-1   Sales Entries

Jan.	3	Accounts Receivable	1,600	
		Sales Revenue		1,600
		Cost of Goods Sold	960	
		Inventory		960
		Sold 8 coats to Paris Clothing Store.		
	5	Accounts Receivable	1,000	
		Sales Revenue		1,000
		Cost of Goods Sold	500	
		Inventory		500
		Sold 5 coats to Extravaganza Clothing Store.		
	11	Cash...	1,568	
		Sales Discounts	32	
		Accounts Receivable		1,600
		Received full payment (within the discount period) from		
		Paris Clothing Store ($1,600 × 0.02 = $32 discount).		
	19	Cash...	1,000	
		Accounts Receivable		1,000
		Received full payment (after the discount period) from		
		Extravaganza Clothing Store.		

E7-2   Accounting for Accounts Receivable

1.   Bad Debt Expense 20,000
                  Accounts Receivable   20,000
            To write off uncollectible accounts in 2006.

2.   Bad Debt Expense 9,000
                  Allowance for Bad Debts   9,000
            To estimate uncollectible accounts as a percentage of the receivables
            (0.04 × $300,000 = $12,000; $12,000 – $3,000 existing credit balance = $9,000).

      Note: When the estimate is based on receivables, the existing balance in Allowance for Bad Debts is considered because receivables relate to sales from all periods. No attempt to match expenses with revenues is made when the estimate is based on receivables.

3.   Bad Debt Expense 1,050
                  Allowance for Bad Debts   1,050
            To estimate uncollectible accounts based on an aging of the receivables.

            Calculation:

0.005	×	$200,000	=	$1,000
0.015	×	70,000	=	1,050
0.030	×	20,000	=	600
0.100	×	8,000	=	800
0.300	×	2,000	=	600

            $4,050
            –3,000   Existing credit balance
            $1,050

E7-3   Accounting for Accounts Receivable

Bad Debt Expense 14,000
      Allowance for Bad Debts   14,000
To estimate uncollectible accounts as a percentage of credit sales ($2,000,000 × 0.70 × 0.01).

Note: When the estimate is based on sales, the existing balance in Allowance for Bad Debts is ignored. The existing balance is related to the previous period's sales and, under a strict interpretation of the matching rule, the 1 percent of uncollectible accounts from this year's sales should be added to it.

E7-4   Assessing How Well Companies Manage Their Receivables

		2005		2006	
1 & 2	Accounts Receivable Turnover	$\dfrac{\$2,000,000}{(\$180,000 + \$300,000)/2}$	= 8.33 times	$\dfrac{\$2,500,000}{(\$300,000 + \$500,000)/2}$	= 6.25 times
3 & 4	Average Collection Period	$\dfrac{365}{8.33}$	= 43.82 days	$\dfrac{365}{6.25}$	= 58.40 days

It appears that accounts receivable collection is getting worse.

E7-5   Accounting For Warranty Expense

1.   Estimated Liability for Service...   12,500
                 Cash...   12,500
            To record cost of actual repairs in 2005.

2.   Customer Service Expense..   75,000
                 Estimated Liability for Service...   75,000
            To record estimated warranty expense based on systems sold.
            (5,000 × 0.30 × $50 = $75,000)

3.   Estimated Liability for Service..   55,000
                 Cash...   55,000
            To record cost of actual repairs in 2006.

4.   Customer Service Expense..   90,000
                 Estimated Liability for Service...   90,000
            To record estimated warranty expense based on systems sold.
            (6,000 × 0.30 × $50 = $90,000)

E7-6   (Expanded material) Foreign Currency Transactions

June 1   Inventory   75,000
                 Accounts Payable   75,000
            Purchased merchandise from Canadian Company.

July 1   Accounts Payable   75,000
            Loss on Exchange Rate Changes..   2,000
                 Cash   77,000
            Paid 100,000 Canadian dollars to Canadian Company costing $77,000.

Chapter 8
Inventory

LEARNING OBJECTIVES

After studying this chapter, you should be able to:

1. Identify what items and costs should be included in inventory and cost of goods sold.

2. Account for inventory purchases and sales using both a perpetual and a periodic inventory system.

3. Calculate cost of goods sold using the results of an inventory count and understand the impact of errors in ending inventory on reported cost of goods sold.

4. Apply the four inventory cost flow alternatives: specific identification, FIFO, LIFO, and average cost.

5. Use financial ratios to evaluate a company's inventory level.

EXPANDED MATERIAL LEARNING OBJECTIVES

6. Analyze the impact of inventory errors on reported cost of goods sold.

7. Describe the complications that arise when LIFO or average cost is used with a perpetual inventory system.

8. Apply the lower-of-cost-or-market method of accounting for inventory.

9. Explain the gross margin method of estimating inventories.

CHAPTER REVIEW

Inventory and Cost of Goods Sold

1. When inventory is purchased or manufactured, it is an asset; when it is sold, its cost becomes an expense (usually called *cost of goods sold*).

2. The cost of merchandise sold is usually referred to as "cost of goods sold" and is deducted from revenues on the income statement. The difference between revenues and cost of goods sold is the gross margin of a firm.

3. A manufacturing firm has three types of inventory: (1) raw materials, (2) work in process, and (3) finished goods.

4. The term FOB (free-on-board) shipping point means that buyers bear the shipping charges, while FOB destination means that sellers bear the shipping charges. These FOB terms are important because the firm paying the shipping costs owns the merchandise during delivery and must include it in its inventory.

5. Goods on consignment are not owned by the seller, and hence should not be included in the seller's inventory. Farm equipment is often sold on consignment. That is, the dealer has physical possession of the equipment and sells it on a commission basis to a customer, but does not own the equipment.

6. Inventory purchased or manufactured during the period is added to beginning inventory, and the total cost of this inventory is known as *cost of goods available for sale*.

Accounting for Inventory Purchases and Sales

7. There are two common methods of accounting for inventories: the perpetual method and the periodic method. Under the perpetual method, the inventory records are adjusted each time inventory is purchased or sold. Thus, at any time, the inventory records should accurately reflect how much inventory is on hand. With the periodic inventory method, adjustments to inventory accounts are made only when the inventory is physically counted (usually at the end of a period).

8. The entries to record inventory transactions under the perpetual and periodic methods are shown in Exhibit 8–1. (Assume beginning inventory was $2,000 and ending inventory is $3,000.)

Counting Inventory and Calculating Cost of Goods Sold

9. Most companies physically count their inventories at year-end. With the perpetual method, the count is confirmation of the amount recorded and a way to reveal shortages. With the periodic method, the count is necessary to determine the amount of ending inventory, and subsequently cost of goods sold.

10. There are two parts to a physical inventory count: (1) quantity count and (2) inventory costing.

11. The calculations for an income statement (through gross margin) are:

   Net sales revenue (gross sales revenue – sales discounts – sales returns)
   - *Cost of goods sold:*
     Beginning inventory
     + Net purchases (gross purchases – purchase discounts – purchase returns + freight-in)
     = Cost of goods available for sale
     – Ending inventory
     = Cost of goods sold
   = Gross margin (net sales revenue – cost of goods sold)

12. An error in the reported ending inventory amount can have a significant effect on reported cost of goods sold, gross margin, and net income. For example, overstatement of ending inventory results in understatement of cost of goods sold and overstatement of net income.

Inventory Cost Flow Assumptions

13. There are four patterns in which inventories can flow through a firm.

Exhibit 8–1   Entries for Periodic and Perpetual Inventory Transactions

Transaction	Periodic Inventory Method	Perpetual Inventory Method

Sale of merchandise	Accounts Receivable (or Cash).... 1,000
	   Sales 1,000
	Sold inventory costing $600 for $1,000.
		Accounts Receivable (or Cash).... 1,000
		   Sales 1,000
		Cost of Goods Sold...................... 600
		   Inventory 600

Sales return by customer	Sales Returns............................... 50
	   Accounts Receivable (or Cash) 50
	Customer returned inventory that
	cost $30 and was sold for $50.
		Sales Returns............................... 50
		   Accounts Receivable (or Cash) 50
		Inventory 30
		   Cost of Goods Sold.................. 30

Purchase of merchandise	Purchases.................................... 700
	   Accounts Payable (or Cash)..... 700
	Purchased merchandise costing $700.
		Inventory 700
		   Accounts Payable (or Cash)..... 700

Purchase return to suppliers	Accounts Payable (or Cash)......... 40
	   Purchase Returns 40
	Returned $40 of merchandise to suppliers.
		Accounts Payable (or Cash)......... 40
		   Inventory 40

Closing entries following physical count of inventory	Inventory 12,900
	Purchase Discounts...................... 60
	Purchase Returns 40
	   Purchases................................. 13,000
	Eliminated beginning inventory balance of
	$2,000 and entered ending balance of $3,000.
	
	Cost of Goods Sold...................... 11,900
	   Inventory 11,900
	Adjustment of inventory account to
	appropriate ending balance.
		No Entry (unless there is shrinkage).

a. Specific identification: The units sold can be specifically identified as being purchased at a certain time.

b. FIFO (first in, first out): The units sold are assumed to be the first inventory items purchased.

c. LIFO (last in, first out): The units sold are assumed to be the last inventory items purchased.

d. Average cost: The units sold are considered to be a mixture of all items purchased.

Just as inventory physically flows through a firm, costs of inventory must also flow through the accounting records in one of the four patterns described.

14. For accounting purposes, if inventory costs remained stable over time, it would not matter which of the above alternatives were used. However, if prices are changing (as they usually are because of inflation and other factors), the alternative used can dramatically affect the amounts a firm reports for cost of goods sold and net income. Specifically, under FIFO the oldest costs become the cost of goods sold; whereas with LIFO the most recent costs become the cost of goods sold.

15. Even though a firm has goods that flow on a FIFO basis, it can use any alternative to flow the costs of the inventory through the accounting records. Many firms have switched to LIFO inventory costing because, in an inflationary environment, it allows a firm to report lower profits, and hence to pay lower taxes.

Assessing How Well Companies Manage Their Inventories

16. Two inventory turnover ratios are used to evaluate how effectively a company manages its inventory. The inventory turnover ratio is calculated by dividing cost of goods sold by average inventory. The number of days' sales in inventory is calculated by dividing 365 (number of days in a year) by the inventory turnover ratio.

17. The number of days' purchases in accounts payable ratio indicates, on average, the amount of time between when inventory is purchased and when it is paid. This number, when compared to the sum of number of days' sales in inventory and the average collection period, provides an indication of the company's cash flow position.

EXPANDED MATERIAL

Further Coverage of Inventory Errors

18. Since, with the periodic inventory method, cost of goods sold is equal to the beginning inventory plus purchases minus ending inventory, an understatement of ending inventory causes an overstatement of cost of goods sold and a resulting understatement of net income. An understatement of beginning inventory has the opposite effect. These errors are summarized in Exhibit 8–2, shown on page 77.

Complications of the Perpetual Method with LIFO and Average Cost

19. While the FIFO inventory costing alternative results in the same reported amounts for inventory and cost of goods sold under either the periodic or perpetual methods, the periodic LIFO and average cost flow alternatives often result in different reported amounts for inventory and cost of goods sold than do the perpetual LIFO and average cost flow alternatives.

Reporting Inventory at Amounts Below Cost

20. When inventory is damaged or obsolete, it should be reported at its net realizable value, which is the amount that inventory can be sold for minus any selling costs.

21. When inventory can be replaced at a price less than its original cost, it must be written down to market. Market price is defined as replacement cost unless that cost is above the ceiling (sales price minus selling expenses) or below the floor (selling price minus selling expenses less normal profit). This accounting for inventory on a lower-of-cost-or-market basis preserves the normal profit margin that will be recognized when the inventory is eventually sold.

Method of Estimating Inventories

22. It is often necessary to estimate the amount of inventory on hand. A common method of estimation is the gross margin method.

23. The gross margin method of estimating ending inventory uses the historical gross margin percentage to estimate the current period's gross margin and then works backward to determine the amount of ending inventory.

COMMON ERRORS

Three common inventory-related errors often made by students are:

1. confusing the journal entries for recording perpetual and periodic inventory transactions,

2. making errors when calculating inventory cost flow assumptions, and

3. not fully understanding the effects of errors on the income statement.

1. The Perpetual and Periodic Inventory Methods

The dictionary defines the word *perpetual* as "unceasing" or "constant." With the perpetual method, you "constantly" (with every sales or purchase transaction) adjust the Inventory account. If you adjust the inventory records for each transaction, then the records should always reflect the amount of inventory in the warehouse. Any shortage must be due to theft, loss, or accounting errors. On the other hand, the dictionary defines *periodic* as "occurring from time to time" or "intermittent." With the periodic method, the accounting records are adjusted "from time to time," namely, at the end of each accounting period so the records can be updated. If you understand the different meanings of *perpetual* and *periodic*, you really should not confuse the two methods. Just remember that, with the perpetual method, inventory must be debited every time inventory comes into the firm and credited every time it leaves the firm. With the periodic method, the inventory records are not adjusted during the period, so other accounts must be used to account for inventory purchase transactions. Those accounts are Purchases, Purchase Discounts, Purchase Returns, and Freight-In.

2. Inventory Cost Flow Calculations

On examinations and quizzes, you will probably be asked to compute ending inventory or cost of goods sold using periodic LIFO, perpetual LIFO, or some other inventory costing method. Because of the similarity of these methods, it is easy to use the calculations for one method while working with another method. The best way to overcome this confusion is to remember the following:

a. With the periodic method, you need not keep track of units on hand during the period. At the end of the period, you simply add total units available, then subtract total units sold to determine how many are left in inventory. If you are using FIFO, the costs assigned to the remaining inventory are those of the last units purchased. If you are using LIFO, the costs assigned to inventory are those of the first units purchased. And, if you are using average cost, an average cost of all goods available for sale is assigned to inventory. There is no need to know when goods were purchased or sold within a period when using the periodic method. In fact, you can assign costs of merchandise to cost of goods sold even though those units were not purchased at the time of the sale.

b. With the perpetual method, you must keep track of purchases and sales within the period, and you assign only the costs of inventory actually on hand to cost of goods sold. Using this method, you progressively work through the inventory records of the period, calculating inventory on hand after every purchase and sale.

It will also help you understand the calculations if you realize that although periodic FIFO and perpetual FIFO methods result in the same numbers, the process of calculation is very different.

3. The Effects of Inventory Errors on the Income Statement (Expanded Material)

The best way to understand the effects of inventory errors is to understand the basic cost of goods sold calculation, which is (with arbitrary numbers):

Net sales revenue		$100,000
Cost of goods sold:		
Beginning inventory..................	$20,000	
+ Net purchases.............................	60,000	
= Cost of goods available for sale..	$80,000	
− Ending inventory........................	(35,000)	
= Cost of goods sold......................		45,000
Gross margin......................................		$ 55,000

If you really understand this calculation, analysis of inventory errors will be easy. This calculation reveals several facts.

a. Cost of goods sold and gross margin are complementary numbers and their total must equal net sales revenue.

b. An over- or understatement of cost of goods sold has the opposite effect on gross margin, and hence on net income.

c. Errors in beginning inventory and net purchases affect cost of goods sold in the same direction (e.g., an overstatement of beginning inventory or purchases overstates cost of goods sold, etc.).

d. Errors in ending inventory have the opposite effect on cost of goods sold (e.g., an overstatement of ending inventory results in an understatement of cost of goods sold, etc.).

e. The ending inventory of one period becomes the beginning inventory of the next period.

Understanding the income statement and cost of goods sold calculations are analytical exercises and must be understood conceptually, not memorized.

Exhibit 8–2   Summary of Errors in Beginning and Ending Inventory

	Beginning Inventory Understated	Beginning Inventory Overstated	Ending Inventory Understated	Ending Inventory Overstated
Beginning inventory	Understated	Overstated	Unaffected	Unaffected
Purchases	Unaffected	Unaffected	Unaffected	Unaffected
Cost of goods available for sale	Understated	Overstated	Unaffected	Unaffected
Ending inventory	Unaffected	Unaffected	Understated	Overstated
Cost of goods sold	Understated	Overstated	Overstated	Understated
Net income	Overstated	Understated	Understated	Overstated

SELF-TEST

Matching

Instructions: Write the letter of each of the following terms in the space to the left of its appropriate definition.

a.	Inventory	**k.**	specific identification
b.	perpetual inventory system	**l.**	net purchases
c.	cost of goods available for sale	**m.**	FOB shipping point
d.	cost of goods sold	**n.**	periodic inventory system
e.	FOB destination	**o.**	raw materials
f.	LIFO	**p.**	work in process
g.	finished goods	**q.**	average cost
h.	consignment	**r.**	lower-of-cost-or-market rule
i.	FIFO	**s.**	ceiling
j.	inventory turnover	**t.**	floor

_____   1.   A business term meaning that the buyer of merchandise bears the shipping costs and acquires ownership at the point of shipment.

_____   2.   Purchases minus purchase returns and purchase discounts plus freight-in.

_____   3.   A method of valuing inventory and determining cost of goods sold whereby the actual costs of inventory items are assigned to specific units of inventory on hand and to those units that have been sold.

_____   4.   Cost of goods sold divided by average inventory.

_____   5.   An inventory cost flow alternative whereby the first goods purchased determine the cost of goods sold and the last goods purchased determine the ending inventory.

_____   6.   An arrangement where merchandise owned by one party is sold by another party, usually on a commission basis.

_____   7.   Inventory ready for resale in a manufacturing firm.

_____   8.   An inventory cost flow alternative whereby the last goods purchased determine the cost of goods sold and the first goods purchased determine the ending inventory.

_____   9.   A business term meaning that the seller of merchandise bears the shipping costs and maintains ownership until the sales destination is reached.

_____   10.   The expenses incurred to purchase the merchandise sold during a period.

_____   11.   Beginning inventory plus net purchases.

_____   12.   A method of recording inventory in which detailed records of the number of units and the cost of each purchase and sales transaction are prepared throughout the accounting period.

_____   13.   Goods held for sale to customers.

_____   14.   A method of recording inventory in which cost of goods sold is determined and inventory is adjusted at the end of the accounting period, not when merchandise is purchased or sold.

_____   15.   Inventory used in the manufacture of products.

_____   16.   Manufactured units not yet finished.

_____   17.   A periodic inventory cost flow alternative whereby the cost of goods sold and the ending inventory are determined to be an average cost of all merchandise on hand at the end of the period.

_____   18.   A basis for valuing inventory at the lower of the original cost or market value (current replacement cost).

EXPANDED MATERIAL

_____   19.   Another name for net realizable value as used in application of the lower-of-cost-or-market rule.

_____   20.   Net realizable value minus normal profit as used in application of the lower-of-cost-or-market rule.

True/False

Instructions: Place a check mark in the appropriate column to indicate whether each of the following statements is true or false.

	True	False

1. During a period of rising prices, firms using FIFO will report higher profits than will firms using LIFO. ......

2. Inventory cutoff refers to the guidelines for properly accounting for inventory at the end of a period. ......

3. Under generally accepted accounting principles, it is necessary for a firm that has a FIFO flow of goods to use the FIFO inventory costing alternative. ......

4. When using the perpetual inventory method, the account Purchase Discounts is *not* used. ......

5. Under the perpetual inventory method, a current record of inventory on hand is maintained. ......

6. A credit entry to the Inventory account is made each time merchandise is sold when the perpetual inventory method is used. ......

7. The cost of shipping merchandise into a firm (freight-in) is added to cost of goods sold for a period. ......

8. Under the average cost—periodic inventory costing alternative, the amount recorded as cost of goods sold is the average cost of all inventory available for sale multiplied by the number of units sold. ......

9. The FIFO cost flow alternative produces the same inventory and cost of goods sold numbers under both the perpetual and the periodic inventory methods. ......

10. In a period of increasing prices, LIFO results in the paying of higher taxes than does FIFO. ......

11. The Inventory Shrinkage account is a real account that is *not* closed. ......

12. A physical count of inventory under the periodic inventory method usually provides only a confirmation that the recorded inventory count is correct. ......

13. With the periodic inventory method, a Cost of Goods Sold account is maintained throughout the period. ......

14. A credit entry to the Inventory account is made each time merchandise is sold when the periodic inventory method is used. ......

15. After all adjusting entries are made and assuming FIFO inventory, the amounts shown as Inventory on the balance sheet and as Cost of Goods Sold on the income statement are the same under the perpetual and the periodic inventory methods. ......

16. With the periodic inventory method, cost of goods sold is calculated as ending inventory plus purchases minus beginning inventory. ......

EXPANDED MATERIAL

17. An overstatement of ending inventory results in an overstatement of net income in the same period. ......

18. An understatement of ending inventory results in an overstatement of net income in the following period. ......

19. When inventory items are included in the ending inventory balance but not recorded as a purchase, net income is overstated. ......

20. When the average cost—perpetual inventory alternative is used, a new average cost must be calculated after each sale of an inventory item. ......

21. In order to use the gross margin method of estimating inventories, the historical gross margin percentage must be known. ......

22. Inventory that is obsolete must be written down to its net realizable value. ......

	True	False

23. The net realizable value of inventory is always equal to the selling price of the inventory. .... _____ _____

24. When inventory is valued at the lower of cost or market, losses resulting from declines in inventory values are recognized before inventory is sold. .... _____ _____

25. During periods of continually rising prices, the periodic LIFO inventory alternative usually provides a net income that is lower than if the LIFO perpetual alternative had been used. .... _____ _____

26. When using the lower-of-cost-or-market method of valuing inventory, floor refers to selling price minus selling costs. .... _____ _____

Multiple Choice

Instructions: Circle the letter that best completes each of the following statements.

1. Which of the following inventory costing alternatives usually results in the highest cost of goods sold amount during a period of continuous inflation?
   a. FIFO
   b. LIFO
   c. Average cost
   d. None of the above

Use the following information to answer Questions 2–5.
Transactions of DEF Company, January 2006

Jan.	1	Beginning inventory	8 snowmobiles at $2,000 each
	5	Purchased	5 snowmobiles at $2,500 each
	13	Sold	9 snowmobiles at $3,000 each
	18	Sold	3 snowmobiles at $3,000 each
	23	Purchased	7 snowmobiles at $2,600 each
	25	Sold	3 snowmobiles at $3,200 each

2. Total sales for DEF Company in January 2006 amounted to
   a. $36,000.
   b. $45,600.
   c. $40,000.
   d. None of the above

3. The total number of snowmobiles available for sale in January 2006 was
   a. 22.
   b. 20.
   c. 18.
   d. None of the above

4. The number of snowmobiles left in ending inventory at the end of January was
   a. 15.
   b. 20.
   c. 5.
   d. 8.

5. The cost of ending inventory using the periodic LIFO inventory alternative was
   a. $12,000.
   b. $12,500.
   c. $10,000.
   d. $13,000.

6. The Cost of Goods Sold account is

   a. an expense.
   b. an asset.
   c. a revenue.
   d. a liability.

7. A Cost of Goods Sold account is

   a. maintained when the perpetual inventory method is used.
   b. debited when merchandise is sold, with the perpetual inventory method.
   c. credited when merchandise is returned by customers, with the perpetual inventory method.
   d. All of the above

8. Which of the following inventory costing alternatives usually results in the highest amount of net income during a period of inflation?

   a. Perpetual FIFO
   b. Periodic LIFO
   c. Periodic FIFO
   d. Both *a* and *c*

9. A firm that has a LIFO inventory goods flow

   a. must use the periodic LIFO inventory alternative.
   b. must use the perpetual LIFO inventory alternative.
   c. must use a FIFO inventory alternative.
   d. can use any inventory costing method.

Use the following information to answer Questions 10–12.
Transactions of DEF Company, January 2006

Jan.	1	Beginning inventory	8 snowmobiles at $2,000 each
	5	Purchased	5 snowmobiles at $2,500 each
	13	Sold	9 snowmobiles at $3,000 each
	18	Sold	3 snowmobiles at $3,000 each
	23	Purchased	7 snowmobiles at $2,600 each
	25	Sold	3 snowmobiles at $3,200 each

10. The cost of ending inventory using the periodic FIFO inventory alternative was

    a. $10,000.
    b. $12,000.
    c. $12,500.
    d. $13,000.

11. The cost of goods sold using the periodic LIFO inventory alternative was

    a. $38,000.
    b. $32,500.
    c. $36,700.
    d. $21,850.

12. The ending inventory using the average cost—periodic inventory alternative was

    a. $12,500.
    b. $10,000.
    c. $11,675.
    d. $12,125.

Use the following information to answer Questions 13 and 14.

Beginning Inventory	$20,000
Purchases	40,000
Purchases Returns	3,000
Purchase Discounts	4,000
Freight-In	?
Cost of Goods Available for Sale	55,000
Ending Inventory	?
Cost of Goods Sold	23,000

13. The amount of Freight-In must be

   a. $3,000.
   b. $4,000.
   c. $2,000.
   d. $1,000.

14. The amount of Ending Inventory must be

   a. $23,000.
   b. $32,000.
   c. $33,000.
   d. $22,000.

15. Which of the following accounts is *not* maintained throughout the period when the periodic inventory method is used?

   a. Purchases
   b. Cost of Goods Sold
   c. Purchase Discounts
   d. Purchase Returns

16. Which of the following is the correct calculation for cost of goods sold with the periodic inventory method?

   a. Beginning Inventory + Purchases + Ending Inventory
   b. Beginning Inventory + Purchases − Ending Inventory
   c. Ending Inventory + Purchases − Beginning Inventory
   d. Ending Inventory + Purchases + Beginning Inventory

17. Net Purchases is equal to

   a. Gross Purchases + Purchase Returns + Purchase Discounts − Freight-In.
   b. Gross Purchases + Purchase Returns + Purchase Discounts + Freight-In.
   c. Gross Purchases − Purchase Returns − Purchase Discounts + Freight-In.
   d. Gross Purchases − Purchase Returns − Purchase Discounts − Freight-In.

EXPANDED MATERIAL

18. When counting its inventory, XYZ Company missed counting $2,000 of merchandise. Because of this error, XYZ's income will be

   a. overstated by $2,000.
   b. understated by $2,000.
   c. correctly stated.
   d. None of the above

19. On December 30, 2006, XYZ Company purchased $2,000 of inventory from ABC Company. Because the accounting department personnel were all on vacation, the purchase was not recorded, even though the inventory was counted during the physical count on December 31, 2006. The result of this error is that in 2006

    a. net income will be overstated by $2,000.
    b. net income will be understated by $2,000.
    c. net income will be correctly stated.
    d. None of the above

20. On December 30, 2006, XYZ Company sold for $2,000 inventory that cost $1,000. Because the accounting department personnel were all on vacation, the sale was not recorded, even though the merchandise was shipped and was not counted during the physical count on December 31, 2006. The result of this error is that in 2006

    a. net income will be overstated by $2,000.
    b. net income will be understated by $2,000.
    c. net income will be understated by $1,000.
    d. net income will be overstated by $1,000.

21. During the physical count on December 31, 2005, XYZ Company did not count $2,000 of inventory. The result of this error is that 2006 net income will be

    a. understated by $2,000.
    b. overstated by $2,000.
    c. correctly stated.
    d. None of the above

22. An overstatement of cost of goods sold results in

    a. no error in the gross margin amount.
    b. understatement of the gross margin amount.
    c. overstatement of the gross margin amount.
    d. None of the above

23. Brown Company sells printers. In its inventory are two printers that cost $200 each and that once sold for $250. Because of recent changes in technology, these printers can now be sold for only $190 and can be purchased for $140. Brown Company should immediately recognize a loss on these transactions. The amount of the loss to be recognized on each machine is

    a. $60.
    b. $10.
    c. $50.
    d. None of the above

24. Jason Company sells calculators. Per-unit information about their model XR-79 calculator is as follows:

Purchase price	$29
Sales price	27
Selling costs	2
Normal profit......................	5
Replacement cost...............	23

    Given this information, Jason Company should value the XR-79 calculator at

    a. $29.
    b. $25.
    c. $22.
    d. $23.

Exercises

E8-1   Cost of Goods Sold

The accountant for Raymond Corporation has just completed the records for the period ending December 31, 2006. These records show an ending inventory balance of $18,700. However, in computing this number, the accountant ignored the following items.

  a. Goods that cost $700 were sold on December 30, 2006. By mistake, these goods were included in the December 31, 2006 inventory balance. The merchandise will not be picked up by the customer until January 3, 2007, and it was counted in the inventory for December 31, 2006.

  b. Merchandise that cost $400 was purchased FOB shipping point on December 30, 2006. Although the purchase was recorded, the goods were not included in the inventory for December 31, 2006.

  c. Goods that cost $500 were sold on January 2, 2007, but were shipped on December 30, 2006. By mistake, these goods were not included in the December 31, 2006 inventory balance.

  d. Raymond Corporation acts as the consignee for suppliers. On December 31, 2006, $4,000 of goods on consignment were mistakenly added in the inventory balance.

  e. The following goods were in transit on December 31, 2006, and were recorded as purchases, but were not included in the inventory as of December 31, 2006.

     (1) Ordered by Raymond Corporation: $600 FOB destination.
     (2) Ordered by Raymond Corporation: $1,000 FOB shipping point.

Instructions:

  1. What is the proper amount of ending inventory as of December 2006?

  2. If purchases (before any adjustments from above) totaled $30,000 and beginning inventory as of January 2006 was $6,000, what is the cost of goods sold in 2006?

Use the following information to complete Exercises E8-2 and E8-3.
During December 2006, Alpha Company (which sells air conditioners and uses a periodic inventory method) had the following inventory transactions and records.

Dec.	1	Beginning inventory	9 units at $400 each
	4	Purchased	6 units at $440 each
	11	Sold	10 units at $700 each
	18	Purchased	4 units at $500 each
	23	Sold	6 units at $800 each
	27	Purchased	2 units at $520 each

E8-2   Periodic Inventory Alternatives

Instructions: Compute both the cost of goods sold and ending inventory balances using the following alternatives.

1. Periodic FIFO inventory alternative

2. Periodic LIFO inventory alternative

3. Average cost—periodic inventory alternative

E8-3   (Expanded material) Perpetual Inventory Alternatives

Instructions: Compute both the cost of goods sold and ending inventory balances using the following alternatives.

1. Perpetual FIFO inventory alternative
2. Perpetual LIFO inventory alternative
3. Average cost—perpetual inventory alternative

E8-4   Closing Entries—The Periodic Inventory Method

Peterson Incorporated, which uses the periodic inventory method, has the following trial balance as of December 31, 2006.

Peterson Inc.
Trial Balance
December 31, 2006

	Debits	Credits
Cash	3,000	
Accounts Receivable	3,500	
Inventory (1/1/06)	12,000	
Equipment	26,000	
Accounts Payable		3,000
Notes Payable		9,200
Capital Stock		14,500
Retained Earnings (1/1/06)		6,300
Sales Revenue		68,000
Sales Discounts	2,100	
Purchases	31,000	
Purchase Discounts		1,000
Freight-In	900	
Salary Expense	9,800	
Rent Expense	7,500	
Income Tax Expense	3,400	
Miscellaneous Expenses	2,800	
Totals	102,000	102,000

Instructions: Given this trial balance and assuming ending inventory of $10,000:

1. Prepare closing entries for the revenue accounts.
2. Prepare closing entries for salary, rent, income tax, and miscellaneous expenses.
3. Prepare entries to adjust the inventory balance and to close the inventory-related nominal accounts.
4. Prepare a post-closing trial balance.

Part 4

Peterson Inc.
Post-Closing Trial Balance
December 31, 2006

		DEBIT	CREDIT

Parts 1 through 3

		JOURNAL				PAGE	
DATE		DESCRIPTION	POST. REF.	DEBIT		CREDIT	

E8-5   (Expanded material) Lower-of-Cost-or-Market Calculations

Market Stores Inc. has the following inventory.

Item	No. of Items	Original Cost	Replacement Cost	Net Realizable Value	Net Realizable Value Minus Normal Profit
A	10	$34	$32	$30	$20
B	12	42	36	46	32
C	8	52	42	62	44
D	6	38	32	68	50

Instructions: Using these data:

1. Compute the amount of inventory that should be reported if the lower-of-cost-or-market rule is applied to individual items.

2. Compute the amount of inventory that should be reported if the lower-of-cost-or-market rule is applied to total inventory.

E8-6   (Expanded material) Gross Margin Inventory Estimation Method

On December 15, 2006, the inventory of Bond Corporation was completely destroyed in a fire. To qualify for reimbursement by the insurance company, the firm needs to estimate the amount lost. The insurance company has indicated that the gross margin method will be an acceptable way to compute the loss. In using this method, Bond Company has obtained the following information.

a. The last financial reports were prepared on October 31, 2006. At that time, the ending inventory balance was $7,200.

b. While all past reports were lost in the fire, Bond has obtained from stockholders the six most recent annual reports. The average gross margin ratio for these years was 38 percent.

c. Suppliers were contacted, and it was confirmed that purchases during the October 31–December 15 period totaled $29,200.

d. Customers were contacted, and it was determined that sales during the October 31–December 15 period totaled $46,000.

Instructions: Estimate the amount of inventory lost in the fire.

ANSWERS

Matching

1.	m	8.	f	15.	o
2.	l	9.	e	16.	p
3.	k	10.	d	17.	q
4.	j	11.	c	18.	r
5.	i	12.	b	19.	s
6.	h	13.	a	20.	t
7.	g	14.	n		

True/False

1.	T	10.	F	19.	T
2.	T	11.	F	20.	F
3.	F	12.	F	21.	T
4.	T	13.	F	22.	T
5.	T	14.	F	23.	F
6.	T	15.	T	24.	T
7.	F	16.	F	25.	T
8.	T	17.	T	26.	F
9.	T	18.	T		

Multiple Choice

1.	b	10.	d (5 units @ $2,600)	17.	c
2.	b	11.	c (7 units @ $2,600;	18.	b
3.	b		5 units @ $2,500;	19.	a
4.	c		3 units @ $2,000)	20.	b
5.	c (5 units @ $2,000)	12.	c (5 units @ $2,335)	21.	b
6.	a	13.	c	22.	b
7.	d	14.	b	23.	a
8.	d	15.	b	24.	d
9.	d	16.	b		

Exercises

E8-1   Cost of Goods Sold

1.
Reported ending inventory amount	$18,700
Item a	− 700
Item b	+ 400
Item c	+ 500
Item d	− 4,000
Item e	+ 1,000
Correct amount	$15,900

2.
Beginning inventory	+	Purchases	−	Ending inventory	=	Cost of goods sold
$6,000	+	$30,000	−	$15,900	=	$20,100
		− 600 [e(1)]				− 600
$6,000	+	$29,400	−	$15,900	=	$19,500

E8-2   Periodic Inventory Alternatives

Units available	21
Units sold	16
Ending inventory	5

Cost of goods available for sale:

Beginning inventory, 9 units at $400 each	$3,600
December 4, purchased 6 units at $440 each	2,640
December 18, purchased 4 units at $500 each	2,000
December 27, purchased 2 units at $520 each	1,040
	$9,280

1. Periodic FIFO Inventory Alternative

   Ending inventory:

2 units at $520 each	$1,040
3 units at $500 each	1,500
	$2,540

Cost of goods available for sale	$9,280
Ending inventory	2,540
Cost of goods sold	$6,740

2. Periodic LIFO Inventory Alternative

   Ending inventory:

5 units at $400 each	$2,000

Cost of goods available for sale	$9,280
Ending inventory	2,000
Cost of goods sold	$7,280

3. Average Cost—Periodic Inventory Alternative

   Average cost:
   $9,280 ÷ 21 = $441.90

   Ending inventory:

5 units at $441.90	$2,209.50

Cost of goods available for sale	$9,280.00
Ending inventory	2,209.50
Cost of goods sold	$7,070.50

E8-3   (Expanded material) Perpetual Inventory Alternatives

Units available	21
Units sold	16
Ending inventory	5

Cost of goods available for sale:

Beginning inventory, 9 units at $400 each	$3,600
December 4, purchased 6 units at $440 each	2,640
December 18, purchased 4 units at $500 each	2,000
December 27, purchased 2 units at $520 each	1,040
	$9,280

1. Perpetual FIFO Inventory Alternative

   Ending inventory:

2 units at $520 each	$1,040
3 units at $500 each	1,500
	$2,540

Cost of goods available for sale	$9,280
Ending inventory	2,540
Cost of goods sold	$6,740

2. Perpetual LIFO Inventory Alternative

Ending inventory:

3 units at $400 each	$1,200
2 units at $520 each	1,040
	$2,240

Cost of goods available for sale	$9,280
Ending inventory	2,240
Cost of goods sold	$7,040

3. Average Cost—Perpetual Inventory Alternative

Average cost:

9 unit at $400 each	$3,600	
6 units at $440 each	2,640	
	$6,240 ÷ 15 = $416	

5 units at $416 each	$2,080	
4 units at $500 each	2,000	
	$4,080 ÷ 9 = $453.33	

3 units at $453.33 each	$1,360	
2 units at $520.00 each	1,040	
	$2,400 ÷ 5 = $480	

Ending inventory:

5 units at $480 each	$2,400

Cost of goods available for sale	$9,280
Ending inventory	2,400
Cost of goods sold	$6,880

E8-4   Closing Entries—The Periodic Inventory Method

1.	Sales Revenue	68,000	
	Sales Discounts		2,100
	Retained Earnings		65,900

To close revenue accounts.

2.	Retained Earnings	23,500	
	Salary Expense		9,800
	Rent Expense		7,500
	Income Tax Expense		3,400
	Miscellaneous Expenses		2,800

To close expense accounts (other than Cost of Goods Sold).

3.	Inventory	30,900	
	Purchase Discounts	1,000	
	Freight-In		900
	Purchases		31,000

To close inventory-related accounts.

	Cost of Goods Sold	32,900	
	Inventory		32,900

To establish ending inventory balance. ($12,000 beginning inventory + $30,900 net purchases – $10,000 ending inventory).

Retained Earnings 32,900
    Cost of Goods Sold 32,900
To close Cost of Goods Sold to Retained Earnings.

4.

Peterson Inc.
Post-Closing Trial Balance
December 31, 2006

	Debits	Credits
Cash	3,000	
Accounts Receivable	3,500	
Inventory...	10,000	
Equipment..	26,000	
Accounts Payable...		3,000
Notes Payable		9,200
Capital Stock..		14,500
Retained Earnings ($6,300 + $9,500)		15,800
Totals	42,500	42,500

E8-5   (Expanded material) Lower-of-Cost-or-Market Calculations

Item	No. of Item	Cost	Market Value	LCM
A	10	$10 \times \$34 = \$\ 340$	$10 \times \$30 = \$\ 300$	$ 300
B	12	$12 \times \$42 =\ 504$	$12 \times \$36 =\ 432$	432
C	8	$8 \times \$52 =\ 416$	$8 \times \$44 =\ 352$	352
D	6	$6 \times \$38 =\ 228$	$6 \times \$50 =\ 300$	228
		$1,488	$1,384	$1,312

1. $1,312

2. $1,384

E8-6   (Expanded material) Gross Margin Inventory Estimation Method

Net sales revenue		$46,000
Cost of goods sold:		
Beginning inventory	$ 7,200	
Purchases	29,200	
Cost of goods available for sale	$36,400	
Ending inventory ($36,400 – $28,520).............	7,880	
Cost of goods sold (62% of $46,000)		28,520
Gross margin (38% of $46,000)...........................		$17,480

Chapter 9
Completing the Operating Cycle

LEARNING OBJECTIVES

After studying this chapter, you should be able to:

1. Account for the various components of employee compensation expense.

2. Compute income tax expense, including appropriate consideration of deferred tax items.

3. Distinguish between contingent items that should be recognized in the financial statements and those that should be merely disclosed in the financial statement notes.

4. Understand when an expenditure should be recorded as an asset and when it should be recorded as an expense.

5. Prepare an income statement summarizing operating activities as well as other revenues and expenses, extraordinary items, and earnings per share.

CHAPTER REVIEW

Employee Compensation Expense

1. Accounting for payroll usually involves several different current liabilities. When salary expense is recorded, the following liabilities are recognized:

Payee	Nature of Liability
Individual employees	Take-home pay
State government	State income taxes withheld from employees' checks
Federal government	Federal income and FICA (Social Security) taxes withheld from employees' checks
Unions, charitable organizations, insurance companies, etc.	Other deductions (usually voluntary) from employees' checks

2. Besides the taxes withheld from employees' checks, employers must also pay unemployment taxes (to both the state and federal governments) and FICA taxes. These taxes—together with those withheld from employees' checks—are paid to the governments on a periodic basis.

3. In addition to current wages paid to employees, there are a number of other employee-related expenses and liabilities that must be recognized. The most common of these are (1) compensated absences; (2) bonus-related liabilities such as stock options and bonuses; (3) postemployment benefits that are paid after an employee ceases to work for an organization but

before the employee retires, such as severance packages; and (4) post-retirement benefits such as pensions, retirement medical insurance, and other benefits.

4. The matching principle requires that all expenses associated with compensated absences be accounted for in the period in which they are earned by the employee. Thus, even though the cost must be estimated, the salary that must be paid for sick days should be accrued by employers.

5. Many companies offer employees bonus plans that provide additional compensation if certain conditions are met. The most common types of bonus plans are additional pay and stock options.

6. The accounting for stock options may be very complicated. The primary complication centers on placing a value on the option. Standard setters have provided two methods of accounting for stock options: the intrinsic value method and the fair value method.

7. The intrinsic value method values the option on the day it is issued. On the date of issue, if the option allows the employee to buy shares at a price that is less than the current market value, then the difference between the option price and the market price on the date of issue is accounted for as compensation.

8. The fair value method attempts to measure the economic value of the option by recognizing that the option may have value in the future depending on changing market values of the underlying stock. Using complex mathematical models, the fair value method recognizes compensation expense based on estimates regarding future stock price changes.

9. Postemployment benefits relate to benefits paid to former employees between the time they leave the company and the time that they are eligible to receive retirement benefits. Those benefits must be estimated in the period in which the employee leaves the company.

10. Costs of providing post-retirement benefits to employees such as pensions and medical benefits must be recognized as a liability over the time the employee works and earns the benefits. The accounting for these benefits is complicated, but you should know that there are two primary kinds of pension plans: (1) defined contribution plan, where the employer sets aside money that will be paid to employees upon retirement (and the payments depend on the earnings of the funds, among other things);

and (2) defined benefit plan, where the post-retirement benefits are paid according to formulas based on number of years worked, salary, and so forth.

11. The financial statement accounts relating to pensions can be divided into two parts: those on the balance sheet and those on the income statement. The balance sheet account can be either an asset or a liability depending on whether the pension plan is underfunded or overfunded. The income statement account can be either a revenue or an expense.

12. The balance sheet account is a combination of two primary measures—the projected pension obligation and the pension fund. The pension obligation is measured by actuaries who consider such things as employee turnover, life expectancy, and salary increases. The pension fund is a function of contributions and returns on those contributions.

13. The income statement account relating to pensions is comprised of three primary components—interest costs, service costs, and return on pension fund assets. Interest costs is the amount of interest accrued each year relating to the unpaid pension obligation. Service costs arise as employees provide more services for the company. The more an employee works, the higher the pension obligation. Service costs and interest costs are offset by the return provided by the pension assets.

14. Postretirement benefits other than pensions are additional benefits promised to employees subsequent to their retirement. These items might include such things as health benefits and life insurance.

Compute Income Tax Expense Including Consideration for Deferred Income Tax Items

15. In addition to payroll taxes, companies are required to pay other taxes to federal, state, and local governments, including sales taxes, property taxes, and income taxes. Sales taxes collected are recorded as Sales Taxes Payable. Taxes on property usually require a year-end adjustment because of taxes owed for the first portion of the assessment year. Income Taxes Payable is the amount expected to be paid to the federal and state governments based on the income before taxes reported on the income statement.

16. Many organizations have a liability on the books called "deferred income taxes payable." This account represents income taxes for which the payment is deferred. There are also deferred tax assets (prepaid income taxes), although much less common. Different income tax liabilities arise because of differences between the income tax laws and the accounting for financial reporting, which create timing differences where income tax expense on the financial statements is more than the actual income taxes that must be paid to the government in the current period

17. One example of when a deferred tax liability results is when an expense is recognized for tax purposes before it is recognized for financial accounting purposes. In the case of depreciation, the tax laws allow for an asset to typically be depreciated faster than is the case for financial accounting purposes. As a result future taxable income will be higher (because of less depreciation in the future) meaning that taxes will be paid in the future. Hence, the deferred tax liability.

18. In the case of deferred tax assets, expenses are typically recognized for financial purposes before they are recognized for tax purposes. Because the expenses are not yet recognized for tax purposes, taxable income is higher in the current period and taxes are paid in the current period knowing that a future deduction will be allowed as the expenses are deducted for tax purposes.

The Difference Between Contingent Items Disclosed in the Financial Statements and Those Disclosed in the Notes

19. There are some operating activities that do not occur on a regular basis, and as most companies hope, never occur. The two most common of these are contingencies and environmental liabilities. Contingencies are liabilities that may or may not occur in the future. The most common example of a contingent liability is a lawsuit (where the company may or may not lose).

20. Contingent liabilities are accounted for differently, depending upon their probability of occurrence. If their occurrence is remote, no disclosure is required in the financial statements. If their occurrence is reasonably possible, they must be disclosed in the notes to the financial statements. If their occurrence is probable, they must be recorded as liabilities in the financial statements.

21. Environmental liabilities are contingent liabilities that present a unique problem: the upper bound on the cost of these liabilities often cannot be estimated. In most cases, environmental liabilities are summarized in the notes to the financial statements.

Capitalize versus Expense

22. It is often difficult to determine whether an expenditure should be capitalized (recorded as an asset) or expensed (recorded as an expense). If the expenditure provides benefits beyond the current accounting period (future benefits), it is normally capitalized; if it benefits only the current period, it should be expensed. Repairs to equipment and research and development costs are examples of items that are difficult to clearly determine whether they should be capitalized or expensed.

Summarizing Operations on an Income Statement

23. A firm prepares an income statement that shows revenues, cost of goods sold, gross margin, operating expenses, income from operations, other revenues and expenses, pretax income, income before extraordinary items, extraordinary items, net income, and earnings per share.

24. Extraordinary items (events that are unusual in nature, infrequent in occurrence, and material in amount) are separated from other revenues and expenses on the income statement because they are not part of normal operations.

25. If applicable, an income statement should provide three earnings-per-share (EPS) numbers: (1) EPS before extraordinary items, (2) EPS on extraordinary items, and (3) EPS on net income. EPS is calculated by dividing these income numbers by the number of shares of stock outstanding.

COMMON ERRORS

Several of the issues discussed in this chapter are quite complex, and we have only scratched the surface. Valuing stock options, computing pension expense, recognizing deferred tax assets and liabilities, and estimating contingencies can each be very difficult. In this chapter we have introduced these topics at a conceptual level so that you would be able to understand the general issues.

A common error made when dealing with pensions is to forget that the pension obligation and the pension fund are combined and disclosed on the balance sheet as one number. The components of the pension are detailed in the notes to the financial statements.

A second common error relates to deferred income taxes. Determining if the difference between financial accounting rules and the tax laws results in a deferred tax asset or a deferred tax liability can be difficult. If the difference results in taxable income being higher than financial income in the initial period of the difference, the result is a deferred tax asset. If taxable income is less than financial income in the initial period of the difference, the result is a deferred tax liability.

A third common error is to expense items that should be capitalized or to capitalize items that should be expensed. Often, significant judgment must be exercised in determining whether something should be recorded as an asset or recorded as an expense.

Another common error is misclassifying accounts when preparing an income statement. When preparing a final income statement, it is important that items be placed in proper categories. For example, cost of goods sold comes before gross margin, selling and administrative expenses are subtracted from gross margin, interest and gains and losses go in other revenues and expenses, and extraordinary items have their own classification.

SELF-TEST

Matching

Instructions: Write the letter of each of the following terms in the space to the left of its appropriate definition.

a. earnings per share
b. pension fund
c. intrinsic value method
d. compensated absences
e. pension obligation
f. extraordinary items
g. income taxes expense
h. post-employment benefits

i. fair value method
j. pensions
k. other revenues and expenses
l. deferred tax asset
m. sales taxes payable
n. contingent liability
o. environmental liabilities
p. deferred tax liability

_____ 1. An uncertain circumstance involving a potential gain or loss that will not be resolved until some future event occurs.

_____ 2. Money collected from customers for sales taxes that must be remitted to local governments and other taxing authorities.

_____ 3. Probable future economic benefit relating to temporary differences between financial accounting standards and the tax law.

_____ 4. Items incurred or earned from activities that are outside, or peripheral to, the normal operations of a firm.

_____ 5. Compensation received by employees after they have retired.

_____ 6. The method of accounting for a stock option when the possibility of future stock price changes is recognized.

_____ 7. Benefits incurred after an employee has ceased to work for an employer but before the employee retires.

_____ 8. The amount of expense related to federal and state government tax laws and typically based on the income before taxes as reported on the income statement.

_____ 9. Nonoperating gains and losses that are unusual in nature, infrequent in occurrence, and material in amount.

_____ 10. The promise to make defined benefit pension payments to employees in the future.

_____ 11. Sick pay and other missed work that must be paid for by employers.

_____ 12. The method of accounting for a stock option that recognizes only the immediate difference between the option exercise price and the current market value.

_____ 13. A large investment of a firm's assets set aside to satisfy obligations associated with a firm's pension plan.

_____ 14. The amount of net income (earnings) related to each share of stock; computed by dividing net income by the number of shares of stock outstanding during the period.

_____ 15. A liability associated with causing environmental damage.

_____ 16. Probable future economic sacrifice relating to temporary differences between financial accounting standards and the tax law.

True/False

Instructions: Place a check mark in the appropriate column to indicate whether each of the following statements is true or false.

	True	False
1. State and federal income taxes are usually withheld from employees' checks.	_____	_____
2. Both the employer and the employee must pay FICA taxes.	_____	_____
3. Compensated absences are usually recognized as expenses when sick days are taken.	_____	_____

	True	False

4. A liability for bonuses payable must be recorded when the target figure or trigger for the bonus has been reached. ....

5. A defined contribution pension plan pays a set amount to employees when they retire, usually based on the number of years worked. ....

6. Sales taxes payable are usually considered long-term liabilities. ....

7. Deferred tax liabilities are much more common than deferred tax assets. ....

8. Taxable income and financial accounting income should be the same each year. .....

9. When taxable income exceeds financial income in the first year of a temporary difference, the result is a deferred tax liability. ....

10. The vast majority of companies in the United States use the "intrinsic value" method in accounting for stock options. ....

11. In accounting for pension plans, companies list the pension obligation and the pension fund assets separately on the balance sheet. ....

12. Return on plan assets is subtracted from interest costs and service costs to determine the pension expense for the period. ....

13. A contingent liability whose occurrence is probable should be disclosed in a note to the financial statements. ....

14. The major difficulty in accounting for environmental liabilities is determining the amount of the liability. ....

15. Expenditures that provide future economic benefits (beyond the current period) should be capitalized, not expensed. ....

16. Recurring gains and losses are classified as extraordinary items on the income statement. ....

17. Extraordinary items are separately classified on the income statement because they are (a) infrequent in occurrence, (b) unusual in nature, and (c) material in amount. ..

18. Earnings per share is equal to net income divided by total assets. ....

Multiple Choice

Instructions: Circle the letter that best completes each of the following statements.

1. Which of the following is *not* usually considered to be a current liability?
   a. Accounts payable
   b. Provision for warranties
   c. FICA taxes payable
   d. Long-term portion of mortgage payable

2. Which of the following taxes is *not* a payroll tax expense of the employer?
   a. FICA taxes
   b. Federal unemployment tax
   c. State unemployment tax
   d. Federal withholding tax

Use the following information to answer Questions 3 and 4.
During the first week of January, Tamara McKeon had gross earnings of $100. FICA taxes are 7.65 percent of wages up to $20,000 for both employer and employee, state unemployment tax is 5.0 percent of wages up to $13,000, and federal unemployment tax is 0.8 percent of wages up to $13,000. Voluntary withholding is $10 (in addition to taxes); federal and state income taxes are $12 and $4, respectively.

3. What amount is the check, net of all deductions, that Tamara received for the week's pay?

   a. $60.55
   b. $65.55
   c. $66.35
   d. $77.85

4. What is the employer's payroll tax expense, assuming that Tamara McKeon is the only employee?

   a. $6.15
   b. $9.55
   c. $8.95
   d. $13.45

5. Accrued expenses for future sick days that will be taken are referred to as

   a. compensated absences.
   b. post-employment benefits.
   c. post-retirement benefits.
   d. current period salary expense.

6. Which of the following is true of defined contribution plans?

   a. Payments are made to retired employees on the basis of years worked.
   b. Payments are made to retired employees on the basis of ending salary.
   c. Payments are made to retired employees based on a fixed formula.
   d. Payments are made to employees depending on the earnings of funds set aside while the employees worked.

7. Deferred income taxes payable are recorded as liabilities when

   a. taxes owed to the government exceed income tax expense in the financial statements.
   b. a company has a net loss on its income statement for the period.
   c. taxes owed to the government are less than income tax expense in the financial statements.
   d. a company has no income tax expense on the income statement but owes the government income taxes.

8. The fair value method of accounting for stock options

   a. compares the option price with the market price on the date the option is issued.
   b. is the method used by most companies in the United States.
   c. is the preferred method backed by the FASB.
   d. is relatively simple to apply when compared to the intrinsic value method.

9. Which of the following items measures the increase in a company's pension obligation as a result of an employee working for an additional year?

   a. Interest cost
   b. Service cost
   c. Pension expense
   d. Return on pension fund assets

10. Which of the following items will cause a company's pension expense for the period to decrease?

   a. Service cost
   b. Return on pension fund assets
   c. Pension obligation
   d. Interest cost

11. A contingent liability whose occurrence is "reasonably possible" must

   a. be disclosed in the notes to the financial statements.
   b. be recorded as a liability.
   c. not be recognized in the financial statements at all.
   d. be recorded as an asset in the current period.

12. Extraordinary items are

    a. unusual types of events.
    b. infrequent types of events.
    c. separately classified on the income statement.
    d. All of the above

13. The earnings per share formula includes

    a. the gross margin amount.
    b. total revenues.
    c. net income.
    d. total expenses.

14. Which of the following is *not* an income statement account?

    a. Sales Revenue
    b. Salary Expense
    c. Purchase Discounts
    d. Accounts Receivable

Exercises

E9-1   Current Liabilities

SOAIS Inc. provides the following information relating to its pension plan

On 12/31/06:

Projected benefit obligation	$1,000
Fair value of plan assets	1,100

During 2007:

Contributions to pension plan	$ 50
Service costs	80
Interest costs	75
Return on pension assets	110

On 12/31/07:

Projected benefit obligation	$1,155
Fair value of plan assets	1,260

Instructions: Compute the following:

1. Net pension asset or liability as of 12/31/06

2. Pension expense for 2007.

3. Net pension asset or liability as of 12/31/07.

E9-2   Preparing an Income Statement

The following information is available for GSM Foods, Inc. for the year ending December 31, 2006.

Income Tax Expense.....................................	$ 48,000
Property Tax Expense...................................	4,550
Miscellaneous Office Expense......................	2,850
Gross Sales Revenue....................................	973,500
Insurance Expense	1,900
Advertising Expense.....................................	7,500
Sales Salaries Expense.................................	113,500
Delivery Expense...	14,800
Sales Returns and Allowances.....................	13,500
Beginning Inventory	120,000
Ending Inventory	145,000
Purchase Discounts......................................	22,000
Office Salaries Expense	50,000
Purchases	700,000
Number of Shares of Stock Outstanding.......	10,000

Instructions: Prepare an income statement for GSM Foods, Inc. for the year ending December 31, 2006, using the form on page 104.

GSM Foods, Inc.

Income Statement

For the Year Ended December 31, 2006

ANSWERS

Matching

1.	n	7.	h	12.	c
2.	m	8.	g	13.	b
3.	l	9.	f	14.	a
4.	k	10.	e	15.	o
5.	j	11.	d	16.	p
6.	i				

True/False

1.	T	7.	T	13.	F
2.	T	8.	F	14.	T
3.	F	9.	F	15.	T
4.	T	10.	T	16.	F
5.	F	11.	F	17.	T
6.	F	12.	T	18.	F

Multiple Choice

1.	d	6.	d	11.	a
2.	d	7.	c	12.	d
3.	c	8.	c	13.	c
4.	d	9.	b	14.	d
5.	a	10.	b		

Exercises

E9-1   Current Liabilities

1. Net pension asset—12/31/06:

Projected benefit obligation	$(1,000)
Pension fund.....................................	1,100
Net pension asset	$ 100

2. Pension expense for 2007:

Service costs......................................	$ 80
Interest costs.....................................	75
Less return on fund assets	(110)
Pension expense for 2007...................	$ 45

3. Net pension asset—12/31/07:

Projected benefit obligation	$(1,155)
Pension fund.....................................	1,260
Net pension asset...............................	$ 105

Also can be computed as:

Beginning balance—net pension asset	$100
Plus contributions	50
Less pension expense..........................	(45)
Ending balance—net pension asset.....	$105

E9-2   Preparing an Income Statement

GSM Foods, Inc.
Income Statement
For the Year Ended December 31, 2006

Gross sales revenue...			$973,500
Less sales returns and allowances..			(13,500)
Net sales revenue			$960,000
Cost of Goods Sold:			
Beginning inventory		$ 120,000	
Purchases	$700,000		
Less purchase discounts...	(22,000)	678,000	
Cost of goods available for sale...		$ 798,000	
Ending inventory		(145,000)	
Cost of goods sold			653,000
Gross margin...			$307,000
Selling Expenses:			
Sales salaries expense	$113,500		
Delivery expense	14,800		
Advertising expense...	7,500		
Total selling expenses..		$ 135,800	
General and Administrative Expenses:			
Office salaries expense	$ 50,000		
Insurance expense..	1,900		
Property tax expense..	4,550		
Miscellaneous office expense	2,850		
Total general and administrative expenses		59,300	
Total expenses			195,100
Income before taxes..			$111,900
Income taxes			48,000
Net income...			$ 63,900

Earnings per share:
$63,900 ÷ 10,000 = $6.39 per share

Chapter 10
Investments in Property, Plant, and Equipment and in Intangible Assets

LEARNING OBJECTIVES

After studying this chapter, you should be able to:

1. Identify the two major categories of long-term operating assets: property, plant, and equipment and intangible assets.

2. Understand the factors important in deciding whether to acquire a long-term operating asset.

3. Record the acquisition of property, plant, and equipment through a simple purchase as well as through a lease, self-construction, and as part of the purchase of several assets at once.

4. Compute straight-line and units-of-production depreciation expense for plant and equipment.

5. Account for repairs and improvements of property, plant, and equipment.

6. Identify whether a long-term operating asset has suffered a decline in value and record the decline.

7. Record the discarding and selling of property, plant, and equipment.

8. Account for the acquisition and amortization of intangible assets and understand the special difficulties associated with accounting for intangibles.

9. Use the fixed asset turnover ratio as a measure of how efficiently a company is using its property, plant, and equipment.

EXPANDED MATERIAL LEARNING OBJECTIVES

10. Compute declining-balance and sum-of-the-years'-digits depreciation expense for plant and equipment.

11. Account for changes in depreciation estimates.

CHAPTER REVIEW

Nature of Long-Term Operating Assets

1. Property, plant, and equipment and intangible assets are assets that are used in the business, are not held for sale, and benefit several periods. Property, plant, and equipment are tangible assets; intangible assets have no physical existence.

2. The major elements in accounting for property, plant, and equipment are:

   a. Accounting for its acquisition.
   b. Accounting for the allocation of its cost over its useful life.
   c. Accounting for expenditures (post-acquisition costs) that either increase its capacity or lengthen its life.
   d. Accounting for the impairment of assets (reduction in the future cash flows to be generated by an asset).
   e. Accounting for its disposal.

Deciding Whether to Acquire a Long-Term Operating Asset

3. Long-term assets such as property, plant, and equipment should only be purchased if they will generate sufficient future cash flows to make the investment profitable.

4. It is difficult to accurately assess how much the future cash flows of an asset will be. When making asset acquisition decisions, future cash flows must be discounted to their present values.

Accounting for Acquisition of Property, Plant, and Equipment

5. Long-term operating assets are originally recorded at cost. When cash is paid for the assets, the cost is the cash given up. When two or more long-term assets are purchased for a lump sum (known as a basket purchase), cost is apportioned by using the relative fair market value method.

6. Sometimes assets are acquired by lease rather than purchase. A lease may be a simple short-term rental agreement, called an operating lease, or it may be substantially the same as an asset purchase. In the latter case, the lease is called a capital lease, and the party acquiring the asset (the lessee) records the asset and liability as if the property had been purchased and financed with long-term debt. A lease is recorded as a capital lease if it meets any one of the following criteria: (1) the lease transfers ownership of the asset to the lessee, (2) the lease contains a bargain purchase option, (3) the lease term is 75% or more of the asset's economic life, or (4) the present value of the lease payments at the beginning of the lease is 90% or more of the asset's fair market value.

7. Assets can also be self-constructed or purchased by acquiring an entire company. Care must be exercised to make sure that appropriate interest and overhead are included in the cost of self-constructed assets. When purchasing an entire company, goodwill is often recorded.

8. The relative fair market value method apportions a lump-sum amount for two or more assets to the individual assets on the basis of their market values. For example, if $200,000 was paid for land and a building with fair market values of $80,000 and $160,000, respectively, the cost would be apportioned as shown below.

Assets	Fair Market Values	Percentage of Total Value	Cost
Land	$ 80,000	1/3*	1/3 × $200,000 = $ 66,667
Building	160,000	2/3**	2/3 × $200,000 = 133,333
Total	$240,000		$200,000

$$* \frac{\$80,000}{\$240,000} \qquad ** \frac{\$160,000}{\$240,000}$$

Calculating and Recording Depreciation Expense

9. Assets become expenses when they are used up or when they are deemed to have no future value. Since plant and equipment assets benefit many periods, their costs are apportioned over their useful lives. This apportioning of the costs of assets is called depreciation for plant and equipment, depletion for natural resources, and amortization for intangible assets. Property (land) is usually not depreciated.

10. The two methods of depreciating property, plant, and equipment that were discussed in the main part of the chapter are: (1) the straight-line method, which charges an equal percentage of the cost to each period benefited; and (2) the units-of-production method, which uses some measure of output to apportion the costs.

11. The salvage or residual value of an asset is an estimated amount for which the asset can be sold at the end of its useful life.

12. The formula for straight-line depreciation is:

$$\frac{\text{cost} - \text{salvage value}}{\text{estimated useful life of asset (years)}}$$

13. The formula for the units-of-production method of depreciation is:

$$\frac{\text{cost} - \text{salvage value}}{\text{total estimated life (units)}} \times \frac{\text{number of units}}{\text{produced during year}}$$

14. As an example of the two depreciation methods, we will assume that on January 1, 2006, TIP Corporation purchased a truck for $65,000. The truck's estimated useful life is 5 years, and its salvage value is $5,000. The truck will be driven 100,000 miles over its life (14,000 miles in the first year, 26,000 miles in the second, 28,000 miles in the third, 12,000 in the fourth, and 20,000 in the fifth). The depreciation for the truck would be calculated as follows.

COMPARISON OF DEPRECIATION METHODS

Year	Straight-Line	Units-of-Production
Basis for formula	5 years	Total units (100,000 miles)
2006	$12,000	$8,400
	$\dfrac{\$60,000\,^*}{5}$	$\dfrac{\$60,000\,^*}{100,000} \times 14,000$
2007	$12,000	$15,600
		$\dfrac{\$60,000\,^*}{100,000} \times 26,000$
2008	$12,000	$16,800
		$\dfrac{\$60,000\,^*}{100,000} \times 28,000$
2009	$12,000	$7,200
		$\dfrac{\$60,000\,^*}{100,000} \times 12,000$
2010	$12,000	$12,000
		$\dfrac{\$60,000\,^*}{100,000} \times 20,000$

*($65,000 – $5,000)

15. The entry to record depreciation expense for the year involves a debit to Depreciation Expense and a credit to a contra-asset account called Accumulated Depreciation. The difference between the cost of an asset and its accumulated depreciation is called the book value of the asset.

16. When a long-term operating asset is purchased during a year, depreciation is taken for a partial year only. The amount of depreciation is usually calculated as a percentage of the year; that is, if an asset is purchased on April 1, nine-twelfths of a full year's depreciation is taken, no matter which depreciation method is used.

17. Long-term operating assets, such as oil wells, timber tracts, and coal mines, are referred to as natural resources, and the process of writing off the costs of such assets is called depletion. Depletion is usually computed on a basis similar to the units-of-production method. That is, a portion of the cost is depleted as each ton, pound, gallon, and so forth is extracted. The formula for computing depletion is:

$$\frac{\text{cost}}{\text{number of tons, pounds, gallons}} = \frac{\text{depletion per ton, pound, gallon}}{} \times \frac{\text{number of tons, pounds, gallons extracted in current year}}{} = \frac{\text{current year's depletion expense}}{}$$

18. Just as a contra account (Accumulated Depreciation) is maintained for property, plant, and equipment, there may also be a contra account

for natural resources. If used, the contra account is called Accumulated Depletion.

Repairing and Improving Plant and Equipment

19. Money spent to improve or repair long-term operating assets is classified as a current expense (ordinary expenditure) if the expenditure only benefits the asset during the current period (such as minor repairs). It is classified as an addition to the asset (capital expenditure) if it provides future economic benefit—that is, if it increases the asset's life or productive capacity.

Recording Impairments of Asset Value

20. Sometimes events occur after the purchase of an asset and before the end of its estimated life that impair its value and require an immediate write-down of the asset rather than making a normal allocation of cost over a period of time. Such decreases in value are called asset impairments.

21. An asset is impaired when the undiscounted sum of estimated future cash flows from an asset is less than the book value of the asset. The impairment loss is the difference between the book value of the asset and the fair value of the asset. Fair value can be approximated using the present value of the estimated future cash flows from the asset.

Disposal of Property, Plant, and Equipment

22. Long-term operating assets can be disposed of in three ways: (1) they can be discarded or scrapped, (2) they can be sold, or (3) they can be traded for new assets. When an asset is scrapped before it has been fully depreciated and no cash is involved, a loss is recognized. When the net sales price of an asset being sold is less than the asset's book value, a loss is recognized; if the net price is more than book value, a gain is recognized.

23. When an asset is disposed of, the entry always involves a debit to Accumulated Depreciation and a credit to the asset account. The other accounts (gain or loss and cash received) depend on the amount at which the asset is sold. The different types of entries are summarized as follows.

Cash (if received)................................. xxx
Loss on Disposal (if net sales
   price is less than book value)............ xxx
Accumulated Depreciation xxx
   Asset .... xxx (cost)
   Gain on Disposal (if net sales
     price is more than book value)...... xxx

Accounting for Intangible Assets

24. Intangible assets are assets that have no physical substance. Common examples are patents, franchises, licenses, trademarks, and goodwill. The process of writing off the cost of intangible assets over their useful or legal lives is called amortization. Most assets are amortized on a straight-line basis, but goodwill is not systematically amortized.

25. Businesses invest in fixed assets to generate a return. The fixed asset turnover ratio provides a measure of how well companies use their fixed assets. It is computed by dividing sales by average total fixed assets for the period.

EXPANDED MATERIAL

Accelerated Depreciation Methods

26. In addition to the straight-line and units-of-production depreciation methods that were discussed in the main part of the chapter, two other common depreciation methods are the declining-balance and sum-of-the-year's-digits depreciation methods. An accelerated depreciation method for tax purposes is called MACRS, which is based on declining-balance depreciation. These accelerated methods provide for a greater amount of depreciation expense in the early years of an asset's life.

27. The formula for the declining-balance method of depreciation (in this example, 200% or double-declining balance) is:

$$\left(\frac{1}{\text{estimated life in years}}\right) \times 2 \times (\text{cost - accumulated depreciation})$$

   Note that the declining-balance method is the only one that does not take salvage value into consideration in the formula. Also, while 2 is used in this formula, 1.5 for 150% declining balance or 1.25 for 125% are also common.

28. The formula for the sum-of-the-years'-digits depreciation method is:

$$\frac{\text{number of years of life remaining}}{\text{sum-of-the-years'-digits}} \times (\text{cost - salvage value})$$

29. Assuming the same facts as in the earlier example (#14), declining-balance (200%) and sum-of-the-years'-digits depreciation calculations would be:

Declining-Balance (200%)	Sum-of-the-Years'-Digits
Double-declining-balance rate $(1/5 \times 2) = 2/5$, or 40%	Sum-of-the-years'-digits $(5 + 4 + 3 + 2 + 1 = 15)$
$26,000 (0.40 × $65,000)	$20,000 [5/15 × ($65,000 − $5,000)]
$15,600 (0.40 × $39,000)	$16,000 [4/15 × ($65,000 − $5,000)]
$9,360 (0.40 × $23,400)	$12,000 [3/15 × ($65,000 − $5,000)]
$5,616 (0.40 × $14,040)	$8,000 [2/15 × ($65,000 − $5,000)]
$3,424* (0.40 × $8,424)	$4,000 [1/15 × ($65,000 − $5,000)]

*Even though $0.40 \times \$8,424 = \$3,369.60$, since $3,424 reduces book value to the salvage value of $5,000, $3,424 is recorded as a depreciation expense.

Changes in Depreciation Estimates

30. Changes in estimates of useful life or salvage value of assets may be required as new information becomes available. Past depreciation amounts are not changed; only future amounts, based on the new estimates, are changed.

COMMON ERRORS

The most common errors made by students in trying to learn the basic material in this chapter involve:

1. Depreciation expense calculations.

2. Expensing amounts for improvements that should be capitalized.

3. Subtracting salvage value from the cost before applying the declining-balance depreciation rate.

4. Exchanges of assets.

---

1. Calculating Depreciation Expense

   The most common error made in calculating depreciation expense is taking a full year of depreciation in the year of acquisition when the asset was used for only part of a year. It is extremely important that you note the date of acquisition before you do anything else.

2. Expensing Amounts for Improving Assets

   If an expenditure on an operating asset will extend the life of the asset, improve the quality or capacity of its output, or alter its use, the expenditure is capitalized and should be included in the asset's cost for use in calculating depreciation in the future. Such costs benefit future periods and should be allocated to future periods through depreciation. They should not be expensed in the period in which they were incurred. Expenses of the period reflect used-up assets, and these improvements have definitely not been used—they will benefit future periods.

3. **Subtracting Salvage Value from the Cost Before Applying the Declining-Balance Depreciation Rate (Expanded Material)**

Remember that salvage value is subtracted from cost in computing depreciation under all depreciation methods except the declining-balance method. For this method, the declining-balance rate is applied to the total cost before salvage value is subtracted. In other words, salvage value is not considered until the end—you do not depreciate the asset below the salvage value.

4. **Exchanges of Assets (Expanded Material)**

Exchanges of similar productive assets are the most difficult exchanges to account for and often confuse students. This is because you have to determine not only whether the assets are similar, but also whether a gain or a loss has occurred. Only then can you record the exchange. Gains and losses are computed by comparing the fair market value of the assets received with the book value of the assets given up. To illustrate, assume that a new truck with a fair market value of $25,000 is purchased for $15,000 cash plus an old truck with a cost of $20,000 and accumulated depreciation of

$12,000. At first glance, the owner of the old truck seems to have lost on the exchange. He is exchanging a truck that cost $20,000 plus $15,000 cash for a truck valued at $25,000. However, he actually gains $2,000, which is computed as follows:

Fair market value received (new truck)		$25,000
Book value given up:		
Old truck ($20,000 – $12,000)...	$ 8,000	
Cash paid	15,000	23,000
Gain realized..............................		$ 2,000

Once you have calculated whether a gain or a loss has occurred, you must remember that gains and losses involve different accounting procedures. Since this exchange of similar assets involved a gain—which cannot be recognized according to the accounting rules—the new asset must be recorded at $23,000, which is the book value of the old asset plus the cash paid.

If the new truck had a fair market value of $22,000, a loss would have resulted, calculated as follows:

Fair market value received (new truck)............................		$22,000
Book value given up:		
Old truck ($20,000 – $12,000)...	$ 8,000	
Cash paid	15,000	23,000
Loss realized		$ 1,000

Since losses are to be recognized, the new truck would be recorded at its fair market value of $22,000.

SELF-TEST

Matching

Instructions: Write the letter of each of the following terms in the space to the left of its appropriate definition.

a.   declining-balance depreciation method
b.   capital expenditure
c.   franchise
d.   intangible asset
e.   sum-of-the-years'-digits depreciation method
f.   amortization
g.   property, plant, and equipment
h.   book value

i.   straight-line depreciation method
j.   units-of-production depreciation method
k.   patent
l.   salvage value
m.   goodwill
n.   depletion
o.   impairment

_____   1.   The process of cost allocation that assigns the original cost of a natural resource to the periods benefited.

_____   2.   An exclusive right granted for 20 years by the federal government to manufacture and sell an invention.

_____   3.   Tangible, long-lived assets acquired for use in the operation of a business and not intended for resale.

_____   4.   An intangible asset showing that a business is worth more than the value of its net assets; equal to the excess of the cost over the fair market value of the net assets purchased.

_____   5.   The process of cost allocation that assigns the original cost of an intangible asset to the periods benefited.

_____   6.   A long-lived asset that does not have physical substance and is not held for resale.

_____   7.   A depreciation method in which the cost of an asset is allocated to each period on the basis of its productive output during the period.

_____   8.   The net amount shown in the accounts for an asset, a liability, or an owners' equity item.

_____   9.   An exclusive right to sell a product or offer a service in a certain geographical area.

_____   10.   A depreciation method in which the cost of an asset is allocated equally over the periods of its estimated useful life.

_____   11.   The estimated value or actual price of an asset at the conclusion of its useful life, net of disposal costs.

_____   12.   An expenditure that is expected to lengthen an asset's useful life or increase its capacity.

_____   13.   A sudden decline in the value of an asset that requires the asset to be written down to its fair market value.

EXPANDED MATERIAL

_____   14.   An accelerated depreciation method in which a declining depreciation rate is multiplied by a constant balance.

_____   15.   An accelerated depreciation method in which book value is multiplied by a constant depreciation rate.

True/False

Instructions: Place a check mark in the appropriate column to indicate whether each of the following statements is true or false.

	True	False
1. Long-term operating assets are assets held for resale.	_____	_____
2. Land is usually considered to be an intangible asset.	_____	_____
3. The relative fair market value method is usually used to allocate the cost of two or more assets when they are purchased for a lump-sum payment.	_____	_____

	True	False

4. A lease is classified as an operating lease whenever the property being leased is a long-term operating asset. ....   _____   _____

5. The residual value of an asset is usually the same as the book value of an asset. ......   _____   _____

6. The straight-line depreciation method usually provides the highest amount of depreciation in the first year. ....   _____   _____

7. Generally accepted accounting principles allow for the expensing of the cost of an asset over a period that is generally shorter than the asset's useful life. ....   _____   _____

8. When money is spent to improve an asset, the expenditure should be capitalized if it either improves the productive capacity of the asset or increases its life. ....   _____   _____

9. When an asset is sold for an amount less than its book value, a gain on the sale is realized. ....   _____   _____

10. Accumulated Depreciation is debited when an asset is sold. ....   _____   _____

11. A contra account called Accumulated Amortization is usually credited when intangible assets are amortized. ....   _____   _____

12. The process of writing off the cost of an intangible asset is referred to as depletion accounting. ....   _____   _____

13. Impaired assets must be written down to their fair market value. ....   _____   _____

14. Net income divided by average fixed assets provides an asset efficiency measure. ..   _____   _____

EXPANDED MATERIAL

15. The declining-balance depreciation method usually provides a higher amount of first-year depreciation than does straight-line depreciation. ....   _____   _____

16. The sum-of-the-years'-digits depreciation method is the only one that does not consider the salvage value of an asset in its calculation. ....   _____   _____

17. A simple formula for computing the denominator in the sum-of-the-years'-digits calculation is: $n(n + 1) - 3$ where n is the number of years in an asset's life. ....   _____   _____

18. Double-declining-balance depreciation (200% declining balance) uses as its basis twice the straight-line rate. ....   _____   _____

19. With the declining-balance depreciation method, one should never depreciate below the salvage value. ....   _____   _____

20. When it can be seen that the estimate of the depreciable life of an asset is in error, all past depreciation charges on that asset should be corrected. ....   _____   _____

Multiple Choice

Instructions: Circle the letter that best completes each of the following statements.

1. Which of the following does *not* apply to intangible assets?
   a. They are capitalized—recorded as assets rather than expenses.
   b. Except for goodwill, their cost is amortized over their lives.
   c. They can suffer an impairment of value.
   d. Their cost is depreciated over their lives.

2. If land and a building with respective market values of $20,000 and $30,000 were purchased for a lump-sum payment of $60,000, the land should be recorded at
   a. $20,000.
   b. $24,000.
   c. $30,000.
   d. $36,000.

3. When entering into a capital lease, the lessee would
   a. debit an asset account for the estimated residual value of the leased asset.
   b. debit an asset account for the total amount of payments required by the lease.
   c. debit an asset account for the present value of payments required by the lease.
   d. make no entry until the first lease payment is made.

4. The cost of an asset less its accumulated depreciation is called its
   a. book value.
   b. residual value.
   c. salvage value.
   d. either *b* or *c*.

5. The entry to record the depreciation expense on a piece of equipment for a year includes a
   a. debit to Accumulated Depreciation.
   b. credit to Equipment.
   c. credit to Depreciation Expense.
   d. debit to Depreciation Expense.

6. The first-year straight-line depreciation expense on an asset with a cost of $42,000, a residual value of $6,000, and a life of 6 years is
   a. $7,000.
   b. $6,000.
   c. $5,000.
   d. $10,000.

7. A truck was purchased for $50,000, is expected to have no salvage value, and has an estimated useful life of 75,000 miles. If the truck was driven 18,000 miles in a year, the units-of-production annual depreciation expense would be
   a. $18,000.
   b. $15,000.
   c. $12,000.
   d. $9,000.

8. The payment for an oil change on a company truck would probably be classified as
   a. an expense.
   b. an asset.
   c. a liability.
   d. either *a* or *b*.

9. The payment for a major overhaul of one of the company's trucks would probably be
   a. expensed.
   b. capitalized.
   c. either *a* or *b*.
   d. neither *a* nor *b*.

10. The entry to record the sale of equipment would probably include a
    a. credit to Cash.
    b. debit to Accumulated Depreciation.
    c. debit to Equipment.
    d. credit to Accumulated Depreciation.

11. Which of the following is *not* true of plant and equipment assets?
    a. They are recorded at cost when purchased.
    b. Their cost is depreciated over their useful lives.
    c. Their value is sometimes impaired.
    d. They are often written up to an amount above cost if they increase in value.

12. Fixed asset turnover measures
    a. the percentage of profit earned on each dollar invested in fixed assets.
    b. the number of dollars invested in fixed assets to generate a dollar's worth of sales.
    c. the number of dollar's worth of sales generated by each dollar's worth of fixed assets.
    d. the number of times during a year that fixed assets move through the firm.

EXPANDED MATERIAL

13. The formula $\dfrac{n(n+1)}{2}$ is used in computing
    a. straight-line depreciation.
    b. units-of-production depreciation.
    c. double-declining-balance depreciation.
    d. sum-of-the-years'-digits depreciation.

14. The highest amount of depreciation will usually be recorded in the last year of an asset's life when using
    a. the straight-line depreciation method.
    b. the sum-of-the-years'-digits depreciation method.
    c. the double-declining-balance depreciation method.
    d. either *b* or *c*.

15. The second-year sum-of-the-years'-digits depreciation on the asset described in question 6 is approximately
    a. $10,000.
    b. $8,571.
    c. $10,286.
    d. $6,857.

16. The first-year double-declining-balance (200% declining balance) depreciation on the asset described in question 6 is
    a. $14,000.
    b. $12,000.
    c. $10,000.
    d. $7,000.

17. Which of the following depreciation methods usually results in the lowest net income in the early years of an asset's life?
    a. Sum-of-the-years'-digits depreciation method
    b. Double-declining-balance (200%) depreciation method
    c. Straight-line depreciation method
    d. 150% declining-balance depreciation method

18. A $10,000 asset that was being depreciated on a straight-line basis is estimated to have no salvage value and a useful life of 5 years. If after 3 years it is determined that the asset would last another 4 years, the amount of depreciation expense to be taken in each of the last 4 years is
    a. $2,000.
    b. $1,429.
    c. $1,000.
    d. $800.

Exercises

E10-1   Acquiring Long-Term Operating Assets

During 2006 Fishkill Company had the following transactions.

1. Purchased a delivery truck for $8,000 cash.

2. Purchased land and a building for $200,000. The fair market values of the land and building are $82,510 and $140,490, respectively. The company paid $20,000 down and borrowed the other $180,000 from a local bank with a promissory note.

Instructions: Journalize these transactions.

JOURNAL PAGE

DATE		DESCRIPTION	POST. REF.	DEBIT	CREDIT

E10-2   Depreciation Calculations

On July 1, 2006, Aspen Manufacturing Company purchased a new helicopter for $1,260,000. The helicopter is estimated to have a useful life of 6 years, or 5,400 hours, and a salvage value of $180,000.

Instructions: Compute the depreciation expense for 2006 using the following methods.
1.   Straight-line depreciation.
2.   Units-of-production depreciation (assuming that the helicopter was flown 600 hours in 2006).

E10-3   Disposal of Long-Term Operating Assets

During 2006, APT Company had the following transactions involving long-term operating assets.

1.   Sold for $4,000 cash equipment that cost $14,000 and had a book value of $5,000.
2.   Took a worn-out, fully depreciated truck that cost $6,000 to the junkyard and received $120.

Instructions: Journalize these transactions.

		JOURNAL			PAGE
DATE		DESCRIPTION	POST. REF.	DEBIT	CREDIT

E10-4   Intangible Assets

On December 31, 2006, ZAP Corporation had the following three intangible assets on its books.

  a. Patent: This patent was purchased from another company on January 1, 2004, for $24,000. At the time of purchase, it was deemed to have a remaining useful life of 12 years.

  b. License: This license was acquired from the U.S. Department of Transportation on January 1, 2005, for $45,000. At the time of purchase, it was deemed to have a remaining useful life of 15 years.

  c. Goodwill: On January 1, 2006, ZAP Corporation purchased the assets of RTC Company for $265,000. It was determined at the time of purchase that the fair market value of RTC Company's individual assets totaled $225,000.

Instructions: Complete the following:

  1. Record the purchase of each asset.
  2. Record the amortization of each asset for 2006.
  3. Compute the book values of these assets on December 31, 2006.

JOURNAL   PAGE

DATE	DESCRIPTION	POST. REF.	DEBIT	CREDIT

E10-5   (Expanded material) Depreciation Calculations

Instructions: Using the data from E10-2, compute the depreciation expense for 2006 using the following methods:

1.   Sum-of-the-years'-digits depreciation
2.   150% declining-balance depreciation

E10-6   (Expanded material) Change in Depreciation Estimate

After 4 full years, Aspen Manufacturing Company (see E10-2) realized that the helicopter would last another 6 years.

Instructions: 1.   How much depreciation expense would the company take in each of those last 6 years? (Assume straight-line depreciation.)

               2.   Record the depreciation expense at the end of the year 2011.

JOURNAL   PAGE

DATE		DESCRIPTION	POST. REF.	DEBIT	CREDIT

ANSWERS

Matching

1.	n	6.	d	11.	l
2.	k	7.	j	12.	b
3.	g	8.	h	13.	o
4.	m	9.	c	14.	e
5.	f	10.	i	15.	a

True/False

1.	F	8.	T	15.	T
2.	F	9.	F	16.	F
3.	T	10.	T	17.	F
4.	F	11.	F	18.	T
5.	F	12.	F	19.	T
6.	F	13.	T	20.	F
7.	F	14.	F		

Multiple Choice

1.	d	7.	c	13.	d
2.	b	8.	a	14.	a
3.	c	9.	b	15.	b
4.	a	10.	b	16.	a
5.	d	11.	d	17.	b
6.	b	12.	c	18.	c

Exercises

E10-1   Acquiring Long-Term Operating Assets

1. Truck 8,000
      Cash.. 8,000
   Purchased a new delivery truck.

2. Building... 126,000
      Land 74,000
        Cash.. 20,000
        Notes Payable... 180,000
   Purchased land and building.

Asset	Market Values	Percent	Cost
Building	$140,490	0.63	$126,000*
Land	82,510	0.37	74,000**
	$223,000	1.00	$200,000

*$200,000 × 0.63
**$200,000 × 0.37

E10-2   Depreciation Calculations

1. ($1,260,000 – $180,000)/6 years = $180,000 per year

   Depreciation for 2003 is $90,000 ($180,000 × ½)

2. $\dfrac{(\$1,260,000 - \$180,000)}{5,400} \times 600 = \$120,000$

E10-3   Disposal of Long-Term Operating Assets

1. Cash... 4,000
   Accumulated Depreciation 9,000
   Loss on Sale of Equipment.. 1,000
      Equipment   14,000
   Sold equipment.

Cost	$14,000	Book value	$5,000
Book value	5,000	Cash received	4,000
Accumulated depreciation............	$ 9,000	Loss..	$1,000

2. Cash... 120
   Accumulated Depreciation 6,000
      Truck   6,000
      Gain on Disposal of Truck   120
   Discarded truck.

E10-4   Intangible Assets

1. Jan. 1, 2004   Patent.. 24,000
                         Cash..   24,000
                     Purchased patent.

   Jan. 1, 2005   License 45,000
                         Cash..   45,000
                     Purchased license.

   Jan. 1, 2006   Assets (Various) 225,000
                      Goodwill... 40,000
                         Cash..   265,000
                     Purchased RTC Company.

2. Amortization Expense—Patent 2,000
      Patent..   2,000
   Amortized patent ($24,000 ÷ 12 years).

   Amortization Expense—License.. 3,000
      License   3,000
   Amortized license ($45,000 ÷ 15 years).

   Goodwill is not amortized, so no journal entry is made for amortization.

3.

	Patent	License	Goodwill
Cost	$24,000	$45,000	$40,000
Amortization	6,000	6,000	--0--
Book value on December 31, 2006	$18,000	$39,000	$40,000

E10-5   (Expanded material) Depreciation Calculations

1. $6/21 \times (\$1,260,000 - \$180,000) = \$308,571$ for first full year
   Depreciation for 2006 is $154,286 ($308,571 \times \frac{1}{2}$)

2. $(1/6 \times 1.5) \times \$1,260,000 = \$315,000$ for first full year
   Depreciation for 2006 is $157,500 ($315,000 \times \frac{1}{2}$)

E10-6   (Expanded material) Change in Depreciation Estimate

Depreciation: $\dfrac{\$1,260,000 - \$180,000}{6} = \$180,000$ per year

Depreciation already taken: $4 \times \$180,000 = \$720,000$

Left to depreciate: $\$1,260,000 - \$720,000 - \$180,000 = \$360,000$

Depreciation per year: $\dfrac{\$360,000}{6} = \$60,000$ per year

2011 depreciation entry:
Depreciation Expense 60,000
   Accumulated Depreciation—Helicopter 60,000
To record depreciation on the helicopter for 2011.

Chapter 11
Long-Term Debt Financing

LEARNING OBJECTIVES

After studying this chapter, you should be able to:

1. Use present value concepts to measure long-term liabilities.

2. Account for long-term liabilities, including notes payable and mortgages payable.

3. Account for capital lease obligations and understand the significance of operating leases being excluded from the balance sheet.

4. Account for bonds, including the original issuance, the payment of interest, and the retirement of bonds.

5. Use debt-related financial ratios to determine the degree of a company's financial leverage and its ability to repay loans.

EXPANDED MATERIAL LEARNING OBJECTIVE

6. Amortize bond discounts and bond premiums using either the straight-line method or the effective-interest method.

CHAPTER REVIEW

Measuring Long-Term Liabilities

1. Money has a time value. That is, since money can be invested and earn a return over time, current dollars are worth more than dollars received in the future.

2. Because money has a time value, its value today is equal to its future value minus the amount of interest that the money could earn. The value today of dollars to be received in the future is called present value.

3. An annuity is a series of equally spaced, equal-amount payments to be received or paid at the end of each period. Because of the time value of money, the dollars paid or received at the various intervals are not of equal value. Therefore, to find the value of an annuity, it is necessary to find the value of all payments on a common date. The present value of an annuity is its value today (when all payments are discounted back to today's value).

4. Conceptually, the amount of a liability is the present value or cash equivalent of all future payments required to pay it off in full.

   a. If a liability is short term, the cash equivalent or present value is usually approximately equal to the stated amount of the debt.

   b. If a liability is long term, paying approximately the market rate of interest, again its cash equivalent or present value is approximately equivalent to the stated amount of the debt.

   c. If a liability is long term, paying either no interest or an interest rate lower than the current market rate, the cash equivalent or present value is less than the stated amount of the debt. In this case, the stated amount of the debt must be discounted to its present value using the market rate of interest.

Accounting for Long-Term Liabilities

5. Money borrowed for a period longer than one year is classified as a long-term liability on the balance sheet. Some common long-term liabilities are:

   Notes payable: Regular borrowing from a bank or other lending institution. Terms, payments, collateral, and other debt requirements are negotiated.

   Mortgage payable: Money borrowed to purchase a specific asset. (Usually the asset is pledged as collateral, and monthly or yearly payments are made.)

   Lease obligations: The present value of money owed on long-term rental of property or equipment. Since such assets are often leased for periods that approximate their useful life, leasing can be essentially equivalent to purchasing.

   Bonds payable: A long-term liability consisting of a periodic interest payment (an annuity) and a repayment of the principal (a lump sum).

6. The most common long-term liability is notes payable. Long-term notes payable are obligations to pay money at future dates at least one year hence.

7. A mortgage payable is similar to a note payable, except that proceeds from a note payable can often be used for any business purpose; however, mortgage money is usually related to a specific asset. Assets purchased with a mortgage are usually pledged as security. Mortgages generally require monthly or periodic payments over the life of the mortgage. During the early years of a mortgage, a large percentage of each payment is interest; in later years, most of the payment reduces the mortgage payable account balance.

Accounting for Lease Obligations

8. A lease must be capitalized if it meets the definition of a capital lease, which generally means that it is a long-term, noncancelable contract to rent property from a lessor. The amount of liability to be recorded in accounting for a capital lease is the present value of all future lease payments (discounted at the market rate of interest). The difference between the present value and the total cost paid on the lease is

charged as interest expense over the lease's life.

9. In those instances where a lease is classified as an operating lease, nothing appears on the balance sheet related to either the asset or the liability. Operating lease obligations are disclosed in the notes to the financial statements and detail the expected lease payments to be made in the future.

The Nature of Bonds

10. Conceptually, the price of a bond is the present value of all future payments required to pay it off in full.

    a. If a long-term bond pays approximately the market rate of interest, its present value is approximately equivalent to the stated amount of the debt.

    b. If a long-term bond pays either no interest or an interest rate significantly lower than the current market rate, the present value is less than the stated amount of the bonds. In this case, the stated amount of the bonds plus the contractual interest rate is discounted to a lower present value, using the market rate of interest. The difference between this lower present value and the face value is called a discount.

    c. If a long-term bond pays interest at a higher rate than the effective (current market) rate, the present value of the bond is more than the stated face value of the bond after discounting the face value of the bonds and the interest payments, using the effective (current) rate of interest. The excess above the face value is called a premium.

Accounting for Bonds Payable

11. Bonds are issued at face value, at a discount, or at a premium. Premiums and discounts on bonds are amortized over the life of the bonds.

12. When bonds issued at face value are retired at maturity, a journal entry is required to close the Bonds Payable account with a cash payment to the bondholders for the face value of the bonds.

13. When bonds are retired before maturity, the typical entry to retire bonds on an interest date (assuming that the entry for the interest payments has been made) would be:

Bonds Payable.................	xxx	
Loss on Bond Retirement.	xx	
Cash............................		xxx

The loss (or gain on retirement) is reported on the income statement as an extraordinary loss (or gain).

Using Debt-Related Financial Ratios

14. Information from the financial statements can be used to assess a company's degree of leverage. Leverage is a measure of the degree to which a company has borrowed money to finance its assets. Three ratios are commonly used to assess leverage:

    a. Debt ratio—total liabilities divided by total assets

    b. Debt-to-equity ratio—total liabilities divided by stockholders' equity

    c. Times interest earned—income before interest and taxes divided by interest expense

EXPANDED MATERIAL

15. Bond premiums and discounts can be amortized in either of two ways: (a) on a straight-line basis, or (b) using the effective-interest amortization method. With the straight-line method, the same amount is amortized each period; with the effective-interest amortization method, the amount varies from period to period.

16. The effective-interest amortization method takes into consideration the time value of money and therefore is theoretically preferred over the straight-line method. With the effective-interest method, periodic amortization is the difference between the cash paid for interest and actual interest expense, which is calculated by multiplying the effective, or real, rate of interest times the bond carrying amount.

17. The amortization of a bond discount increases interest expense, whereas the amortization of a bond premium decreases interest expense. This amortization of premiums and discounts accounts for the difference between the effective rate and the stated rate on bonds. The following hypothetical journal entries for the amortization of a bond discount and a bond premium illustrate the effect on interest expense.

Bond Interest Expense......	5,200	
Discount on Bonds		200
Cash.............................		5,000

Bond Interest Expense......	4,800	
Premium on Bonds...........	200	
Cash.............................		5,000

COMMON ERRORS

The most common errors and most difficult areas to understand in this chapter are:

1. The discounting of long-term liabilities.

2. The accounting for leases.

3. Miscalculating the issuance price of the bond.

4. Miscalculating the amortization of the premium or the discount.

---

1. **Discounting of Long-Term Liabilities**

   It is sometimes very difficult to understand conceptually why long-term liabilities must often be discounted. To help you understand, think of liabilities this way. Suppose you were buying a new car. You went to one dealer and he offered you the car for $12,000, including a $2,000 down payment and 13 percent interest on the balance, to be paid over a period of 4 years. The second dealer advertised 4 percent interest, but upon visiting that dealership you found that the car could only be purchased for $14,000, including a $2,000 down payment and the balance at 4 percent over 4 years. The final dealer offered an even better deal—no interest on the unpaid balance. You couldn't believe it; however, when you visited that dealer, you found that he would only sell the car for $16,000. What is really happening? Probably all the dealers are charging approximately 13 percent interest, but the last two are hiding part or all of the interest in the purchase price.

   Because of the potential for this kind of abuse, accounting rule makers have decided that for liabilities where there is either no interest or an unreasonably low interest rate, part of the liability is really interest. If they didn't impose this requirement, debt would often be disclosed without associated interest expense, and net income would be artificially high.

   Because the calculations and entries required for discounted liabilities are difficult, it is very important that you read carefully the section of the chapter dealing with the measurement of liabilities.

2. **The Accounting for Leases**

   The only exposure most of you have to leases is the apartment lease you sign for one year at a time. The term is short, and you will not have any financial interest in the apartment at the conclusion of the lease; you are merely renting under a fixed rental agreement. These rental-type leases differ from a lease where the lessee has the leased asset for most of its useful life or where it is purchased for a nominal amount at the end of the lease term. This latter kind of lease is very much like a purchase, and so it must be capitalized—recorded as both an asset and a liability. And, since this type of lease is similar to a "noninterest-bearing note," it is recorded at its discounted present value. Then as each lease payment is made, part of it is interest and part is a reduction of the lease liability. Similarly, since the leased asset is "owned," it must be depreciated (amortized) over the lease period. Don't let the term lease confuse you. Rather, think of a lease as either a rental agreement (noncapitalizable lease) or as a non-interest-bearing note payable (capitalized lease).

3. The Bond Issuance Price

The issuance price is often miscalculated because the wrong number of periods is used in computing the present value, because the cash interest payments used in the calculation are wrong, or because the interest rate used in discounting the principal and interest is incorrect.

a. Bonds usually are based on semiannual compounding. This means that a 10-year bond will have 20 interest payments. Therefore, as a general rule, the number of periods you use in determining a bond's present value will be double its life (a 5-year bond will have 10 periods, a 20-year bond will have 40 periods, and so on).

b. The cash interest payments are based on the stated (contract) rate of the interest, not on the effective rate. For example, if a $100,000 bond has a stated rate of 8 percent and an effective rate of 10 percent, the cash payments will be $8,000 per year (8% × $100,000), or $4,000 every 6 months. Do not use $10,000 (10% × $100,000), and be sure to remember that the interest is paid twice a year at half the stated rate times the face value of the bonds (for example, 4% × $100,000 = $4,000).

c. In computing the issuance price of a bond, the principal and the interest payments are discounted at the effective rate, not the stated (contract) rate. Since the compounding is semiannual, the principal and the interest must be discounted for the number of semiannual periods (see a.) at the 6-months' effective rate. Thus, a $100,000, 10-year bond with a contract rate of 8 percent and an effective rate of 10 percent would be discounted for 20 periods at 5%.

To illustrate the correct computation of the issuance price of a bond, assume that $200,000 face value bonds with a 5-year life and a stated rate of 10 percent are issued on January 1, when the effective rate of interest is 12 percent. To calculate the issuance price, you first determine the following facts:

a. The principal is $200,000.

b. The semiannual interest payments are $10,000 (5% × $200,000), payable January 1 and July 1.

c. The number of amortization periods is 10 (5 years × 2).

d. The discount rate is 6 percent (12% ÷ 2).

e. The present value factor to discount the principal of $200,000 is 0.5584 (see Table I on text page 475—6 percent for 10 periods). *Note*: Do not use the stated rate in determining the present value factor.

f. The present value factor to discount the interest payments of $10,000 is 7.3601 (see Table II—6 percent for 10 periods). *Note*: Do not use 5 percent or 5 periods.

Based on this information, the issuance price of the bonds would be computed as follows:

Discounting the principal:
$200,000 × 0.5584 .... $111,680
Discounting the interest payments:
$10,000 × 7.3601 73,601
Issuance price (total present value) . $185,281

4. The Amortization of a Bond Premium or a Discount (Expanded material)

The premium or discount can be amortized using either the straight-line or the effective-interest method. When straight-line amortization is used and the bond is issued on an interest date, the annual amortization is equal to the premium or the discount divided by the number of amortization periods for which the bonds will be outstanding. Thus, for the $200,000, 10 percent, 5-year bonds issued at $185,281, the discount would be $14,719 ($200,000 − $185,281). The amortization periods would be 10 (5 years × 2), and the semiannual amortization would be $1,472 ($14,719 ÷ 10). The amortization for a full calendar year would be $2,944 ($14,719 ÷ 5). If the bonds had been dated and issued on April 1 and the corporation was on a calendar-year basis, the amortization for the first year would be $2,208 ($2,944 × 9/12).

If the bonds were dated on January 1 but not issued until April 1, the amortization period would be 4 years and 9 months (57 months). In this case, it is usually best to compute the amortization on a monthly basis ($14,719 discount ÷ 57 months = $258.23) and then multiply by the number of months that the discount (or premium) is to be amortized in that year. Thus, if the monthly amortization is $258.23 and the bonds were issued on April 1, the amortization the first year would be $2,324 ($258.23 × 9), and the amortization the second year would be $3,099 ($258.23 × 12).

When effective-interest amortization is used and the bonds are issued on an interest date, the amount of the premium or the discount to be amortized each 6-month period is the difference between the effective-interest amount and the actual interest paid for the 6-month period. To illustrate, assume that the issuance price of the $200,000 face value, 5-year, 10 percent bonds described above was $185,281. With an effective-interest rate of 12 percent, the effective interest for the first 6 months would be $11,117 ($185,281 × 12% × 1/2 year). The actual interest paid would be $10,000 ($200,000 × 10% × 1/2 year). Therefore, the discount to

be amortized would be $1,117 ($11,117 − $10,000). Remember that the purpose of the amortization is to move the carrying value of the bond toward its face value by the bond's maturity date and to reflect the interest expense at the effective rate, not the stated rate. Thus, using effective-interest amortization, the entry for reporting the interest expense and the bond discount amortization for the $200,000 bond issue would be:

Bond Interest Expense......	11,117	
Discount on Bonds		1,117
Cash..............................		10,000

After this entry is made, the carrying value of the bond would be $186,398 ($185,281 + $1,117), which can be verified by discounting the face value and the interest payments for one less period than was used for determining the issuance price of $185,281.

If the bonds were dated January 1 and issued on April 1, you would use a similar procedure, except that you would use the April 1 issuance price to determine the effective interest for the 3-month period ending June 30.

SELF-TEST

Matching

Instructions: Write the letter of each of the following terms in the space to the left of its appropriate definition.

a. annuity
b. term bonds
c. lessee
d. debt ratio
e. note payable
f. present value
g. market rate of interest
h. debt-to-equity ratio
i. stated rate of interest
j. callable bonds
k. debentures

l. convertible bonds
m. serial bonds
n. times interest earned
o. bond premium
p. effective-interest amortization
q. bond discount
r. straight-line amortization
s. lessor
t. face value
u. bond payable

_____ 1. An entity that agrees to make periodic rental payments for the use of leased property.

_____ 2. A debt owed to a creditor, evidenced by an unconditional written promise to pay a sum of money on or before a specified future date.

_____ 3. Bonds that all mature on one day.

_____ 4. A landlord or owner of leased property.

_____ 5. A measure of the amount of assets provided by lenders.

_____ 6. The value today of money to be received at some future date, given a specified interest rate.

_____ 7. A series of equal amounts to be received or paid at the end of equal time intervals.

_____ 8. The nominal amount printed on the face of a bond.

_____ 9. A long-term debt, evidenced by an unconditional written promise to pay interest regularly plus a sum of money on a specified future date.

_____ 10. A measure of the balance of funds provided by creditors and stockholders.

_____ 11. The actual rate of return earned or paid on a bond.

_____ 12. Bonds that mature in a series of installments.

_____ 13. Bonds that can be redeemed by the issuer over specified periods before maturity at a designated price.

_____ 14. Bonds that have no specific assets as security to guarantee payment.

_____ 15. The rate of interest specified on the bond indenture to be paid annually to a bondholder.

_____ 16. Bonds that can be converted to other securities, such as stocks, after a specified period, at the option of the bondholder.

_____ 17. The difference between the face value and the sales price when bonds are sold above their face value.

_____ 18. A ratio of the income available for interest payments to the annual interest expense.

_____ 19. The difference between the face value and the sales price when bonds are sold below their face value.

EXPANDED MATERIAL

_____ 20. A method of systematically writing off a bond premium or discount that takes into consideration the time value of money; results in an equal rate of interest for each period.

_____ 21. A method of systematically writing off a bond premium or discount, resulting in an equal amount being amortized each period.

True/False

Instructions: Place a check mark in the appropriate column to indicate whether each of the following statements is true or false.

	True	False
1. The formula for computing interest on a note is: Principal × interest rate × time (fraction of a year).	_____	_____
2. The present value of a long-term liability is usually greater than the stated amount of the liability.	_____	_____
3. A note payable is a written promise to pay a stated amount of money in the future.	_____	_____
4. During the early years of a mortgage, most of the mortgage payment goes toward reducing the principal mortgage balance.	_____	_____
5. A person or company leasing an asset from another company is called a lessor.	_____	_____
6. A lease that is essentially equivalent to a purchase must be recorded both as an asset and as a liability.	_____	_____
7. Interest expense on a lease is usually recognized on a straight-line basis.	_____	_____
8. All leases must be capitalized.	_____	_____
9. Coupon bonds and callable bonds are the same thing.	_____	_____
10. Because interest expense is tax deductible, the real cost of borrowing money by issuing bonds (in a profitable company) is less than the stated rate of interest.	_____	_____
11. The bond principal is the same as the face value of a bond.	_____	_____
12. The issuance price of bonds is usually a function of the stability of the organization issuing the bonds and the stated interest rate on the bonds.	_____	_____
13. A bond carrying a stated rate of interest that is lower than the market rate will usually sell for a premium.	_____	_____
14. The effective interest rate is less than the stated rate when bonds sell at a discount.	_____	_____

EXPANDED MATERIAL

	True	False
15. The Discount on Bonds account is a contra-long-term liability account.	_____	_____
16. The amortization of a bond premium reduces the amount of interest expense.	_____	_____
17. The effective-interest amortization method is preferred to the straight-line method by the FASB.	_____	_____
18. When a bond discount is amortized, the carrying value of the bond decreases.	_____	_____
19. When bonds are sold at a discount, the effective rate of interest is higher than the stated rate.	_____	_____

Multiple Choice

Instructions: Circle the letter that best completes each of the following statements.

1. Which of the following is a characteristic of a mortgage payable?
   a. The liability is usually secured with some kind of collateral.
   b. The liability usually requires regular periodic repayments.
   c. The liability is usually evidenced by a mortgage document.
   d. All of the above

2. The balances in the Leased Asset and Lease Liability accounts will be equal
   a. throughout the life of the lease.
   b. never.
   c. at the inception of the lease.
   d. at the end of each year during the lease term.

3. An investor who thought a company would be extremely profitable in the future and that the company's stock price would increase significantly would be most interested in which of the following?

   a. Secured bonds
   b. Serial bonds
   c. Callable bonds
   d. Convertible bonds

4. Bonds payable must be discounted to their present value for balance sheet presentation when

   a. they are issued between interest dates at par.
   b. the bonds' stated rate of interest equals the market rate of interest.
   c. the bonds' stated rate of interest is less than the market rate of interest.
   d. Both *b* and *c*

5. If the market rate of interest is 12 percent and a company issues 10 percent long-term bonds, what interest rate would be used in the tables to discount the bonds (assuming semiannual compounding)?

   a. 6 percent
   b. 5 percent
   c. 10 percent
   d. 12 percent

6. The effective interest rate will be lower than the stated interest rate

   a. if bonds are sold at a premium.
   b. if bonds are sold at a discount.
   c. if bonds are sold at par.
   d. at no time.

7. The effective rate of interest on bonds would be higher than the stated rate if

   a. bonds sold at par.
   b. bonds sold at a premium.
   c. bonds sold at a discount.
   d. bonds sold at face value.

8. Assume the market interest rate of 12 percent. Bonds that have a stated interest rate of 10 percent will probably be issued at

   a. a discount.
   b. par.
   c. a premium.
   d. face value.

EXPANDED MATERIAL

9. The account Discount on Bonds is credited

   a. when bonds are issued at a discount.
   b. when a bond discount is amortized.
   c. Both *a* and *b*
   d. Neither *a* nor *b*

10. The amortization of a bond discount

   a. increases bond interest expense.
   b. decreases bond interest expense.
   c. has no effect on bond interest expense.
   d. does not always have the same effect on interest expense.

11. Bond premiums and discounts are amortized
    a. over their legal life.
    b. only over the period the bonds are outstanding.
    c. only by the investor and not the issuer.
    d. only by the issuer and not the investor.

12. When the effective-interest amortization method is used, interest expense is equal to the

    a. bond carrying value times the stated interest rate.
    b. bond carrying value times the effective interest rate.
    c. bond principal times the effective interest rate.
    d. bond principal times the stated interest rate.

13. The entry to pay interest and amortize a bond premium includes a

    a. debit to Premium on Bonds.
    b. credit to Premium on Bonds.
    c. credit to Interest Expense.
    d. debit to Interest Revenue.

14. If bonds originally issued at a premium are retired before maturity at a gain, the entry to record the retirement includes

    a. a debit to Gain on Sale and a credit to Premium on Bonds.
    b. a credit to Gain on Sale and a credit to Premium on Bonds.
    c. a credit to Gain on Sale and a debit to Premium on Bonds.
    d. None of the above

Exercises

E11-1   Notes Payable

On December 15, 2006, Audubon Company borrowed $21,000 for 60 days from Second National City Bank at 12 percent interest. Assume that Audubon's accounting period ends on December 31.

Instructions: Make the necessary journal entries to account for the note on the following dates (use a 365-day year):
1. December 15, 2006
2. December 31, 2006
3. February 13, 2007 (payment date).

JOURNAL   **PAGE**

DATE		DESCRIPTION	POST. REF.	DEBIT	CREDIT

E11-2   Mortgages Payable

Assume that a company signs a mortgage agreement to borrow $150,000 to build an addition to its research lab. The company pledges the lab as collateral for the loan. The mortgage is for 20 years at 12 percent, and the annual payment is $20,081.93 (150,000/7.4694 [Table II] = 20,081.93).

Instructions: Prepare the entries to record the acquisition of the mortgage and the first annual payment.

JOURNAL   **PAGE**

DATE		DESCRIPTION	POST. REF.	DEBIT	CREDIT

E11-3 Lease Accounting

Ledbetter Company leased a computer for 10 years from Diamond Corporation. The fair market value of the computer is $94,528, which is equal to the present value of the lease payments. The annual lease payment is $17,000.

Instructions: 1. Record the lease, assuming that it should be capitalized.
2. Record the annual payment of the lease and interest expense (assuming 12 percent interest) and the amortization (depreciation) expense, using the straight-line method of amortization.
3. Record the annual lease payment, assuming that the lease does not need to be capitalized.

JOURNAL   **PAGE**

DATE	DESCRIPTION	POST. REF.	DEBIT	CREDIT

E11-4   Retirement of Bonds at Maturity

Bedford Corporation had 5-year bonds outstanding at December 31, 2006, as follows.

Bonds payable (10%)......................	$240,000
Bond premium	3,000
Total liability	$243,000

The bonds were issued on July 1, 2002, and pay interest on January 1 and July 1. They mature on July 1, 2007. The premium has been amortized on a straight-line basis.

Instructions: 1. What was the total bond premium when the bonds were issued?

2. At the issuance date, was the effective interest rate higher or lower than the stated rate?

3. Prepare the journal entries that would be made to retire the bonds on July 1, 2007.

	JOURNAL			PAGE	
DATE	DESCRIPTION	POST. REF.	DEBIT		CREDIT

E11-5   (Expanded material) Accounting for Bonds Payable (Straight-Line)

On January 1, 2005, ABC Company authorized $200,000 of 20-year, 10 percent bonds. Because of a tight money market, these bonds (which are to pay interest annually on January 1) were not issued until November 1, 2005, when they were sold at 111 1/2.

Instructions: Using the straight-line method of amortization, prepare journal entries to record the following:
1. The authorization of the bonds on January 1, 2005
2. The issuance of the bonds on November 1, 2005
3. The December 31, 2005 adjusting entry
4. The January 1, 2006 annual payment of interest
5. The December 31, 2006 adjusting entry

JOURNAL   **PAGE**

DATE	DESCRIPTION	POST. REF.	DEBIT	CREDIT

E11-6   (Expanded material) Effective-Interest Amortization

Mississippi River Company issued an 8 percent, $1,000, 4-year bond on January 1, 2006. The interest is payable each year on December 31. The bond was sold at an effective interest rate of 10 percent. The following (rounded) computations have been made.

Date	Cash	Interest	Amortization	Balance
Jan. 1, 2006				$ 937
Dec. 31, 2006	$80	$94	$14	951
Dec. 31, 2007	80	95	15	966
Dec. 31, 2008	80	97	17	983
Dec. 31, 2009	80	97	17	1,000

Instructions: 1. At what price was the bond issued?

2. Did the bond sell at a premium or a discount?

3. How much interest was paid each year on the bond?

4. How much interest expense would be shown on the income statement in 2008?

5. Which method of amortization was used?

ANSWERS

Matching

1.	c	8.	t	15.	i
2.	e	9.	u	16.	l
3.	b	10.	h	17.	o
4.	s	11.	g	18.	n
5.	d	12.	m	19.	q
6.	f	13.	j	20.	p
7.	a	14.	k	21.	r

True/False

1.	T	8.	F	14.	F
2.	F	9.	F	15.	T
3.	T	10.	T	16.	T
4.	F	11.	T	17.	T
5.	F	12.	T	18.	F
6.	T	13.	F	19.	T
7.	F				

Multiple Choice

1.	d	6.	a	11.	b
2.	c	7.	c	12.	b
3.	d	8.	a	13.	a
4.	c	9.	b	14.	c
5.	a	10.	a		

Exercises

E11-1   Notes Payable

1. Dec. 15, 2006   Cash 21,000
                         Notes Payable 21,000
                    Borrowed $21,000 from Second National City Bank.

2. Dec. 31, 2006   Interest Expense 110
                         Interest Payable 110
                    To record the interest expense on note to Second National
                    City Bank for 16 days ($21,000 × 0.12 × 16/365 = $110).

3. Feb. 13, 2007   Interest Expense 304
   (payment date)   Interest Payable 110
                    Note Payable 21,000
                         Cash 21,414
                    Paid $21,000 note to Second National City Bank
                    ($21,000 × 0.12 × 60/365 = $414; $414 – $110 = $304).

E11-2   Mortgages Payable

Acquisition of Mortgage:

Cash 150,000

   Mortgage Payable 150,000

Borrowed $150,000 to build an addition to the research lab.

First Annual Payment:

Mortgage Payable 2,081.93

Interest Expense 18,000.00

   Cash 20,081.93

To make the first annual mortgage payment on the addition
to the research lab ($150,000 × 0.12 = $18,000).

E11-3   Lease Accounting

1. Leased Computer 94,528

   Lease Liability 94,528

To record 10-year lease of a computer (discounted at 12%).

2. Lease Liability 5,657

   Interest Expense 11,343

     Cash 17,000

Paid for first year of lease of computer
($94,528 × 0.12 = $11,343; $17,000 − $11,343 = $5,657).

   Amortization (Depreciation) Expense 9,453

     Accumulated Amortization (Depreciation)—Leased Computer 9,453

To record amortization on leased computer for the first year
($94,528/10 = $9,453).

3. Rent Expense 17,000

   Cash 17,000

To record annual lease expense on computer.

E11-4   Retirement of Bonds at Maturity

1. $3,000 × 10 periods = $30,000.

2. The effective rate was lower than 10 percent, since the bonds sold at a premium.

3. Entries on July 1, 2007:

   Bond Interest Expense 9,000

   Premium on Bonds 3,000

     Cash 12,000

Paid interest on bonds and amortized the bond premium.

   Bonds Payable 240,000

     Cash 240,000

To retire bonds at maturity.

E11-5   (Expanded material) Accounting for Bonds Payable (Straight-Line)

1. No entry.

2. Cash.. 239,667
      Premium on Bonds   23,000
      Bonds Payable   200,000
      Bond Interest Payable...   16,667
    Issued $200,000 bonds at 111 1/2 (Premium: $200,000 × 11 1/2% = $23,000;
    Accrued interest: $200,000 × 0.10 × 5/6 = $16,667).

3. Bond Interest Payable... 16,667
    Bond Interest Expense... 3,133
    Premium on Bonds 200
      Bond Interest Payable...   20,000
    To record annual interest expense on bonds.
    (Premium amortization is $23,000 ÷ 230 months = $100 per month.)
    ($200,000 × 0.10 × 1/6 = $3,333) ($3,333 – $200 = $3,133)

4. Bond Interest Payable... 20,000
      Cash..   20,000
    Paid annual interest on bonds.

5. Bond Interest Expense... 18,800
    Premium on Bonds 1,200
      Bond Interest Payable...   20,000
    To record annual interest expense on bonds.

E11-6   (Expanded material) Effective-Interest Amortization

1. The bond was issued at $937.

2. The bond sold at a discount.

3. Interest of $80 was paid each year.

4. Interest expense of $97 would be shown on the income statement in 2008.

5. The effective-interest amortization method was used since the interest expense is not identical for all years.

Chapter 12
Equity Financing

LEARNING OBJECTIVES

After studying this chapter, you should be able to:

1. Distinguish between debt and equity financing and describe the advantages and disadvantages of organizing a business as a proprietorship or a partnership.

2. Describe the basic characteristics of a corporation and the nature of common and preferred stock.

3. Account for the issuance and repurchase of common and preferred stock.

4. Understand the factors that impact retained earnings, describe the factors determining whether a company can and should pay cash dividends, and account for cash dividends.

5. Describe the purpose of reporting comprehensive income in the equity section of the balance sheet and prepare a statement of stockholders' equity.

EXPANDED MATERIAL LEARNING OBJECTIVES

6. Account for stock dividends and distinguish them from stock splits.

7. Explain prior-period adjustments and prepare a statement of retained earnings.

CHAPTER REVIEW

Raising Equity Financing

1. When companies obtain money by borrowing from financial institutions or by issuing bonds, it is called debt financing. When companies raise money by selling stock, it is called equity financing. Debt financing results in liabilities on the balance sheet; equity financing transactions affect the stockholders' equity section of the balance sheet.

2. There are three different types of business organizations: (a) proprietorships, (b) partnerships, and (c) corporations. A proprietorship is an unincorporated business owned by one person. A partnership is an unincorporated business owned by two or more persons or entities. A major disadvantage of proprietorships and partnerships is the unlimited liability of the owner or partners.

3. A corporation is an entity, distinct from its owners, that can conduct business, sue, and enter into contracts. Stockholders are held responsible for the debts and actions of a corporation only to the extent of their investment.

4. Corporations are given life (incorporated) by a state and have a continuity of existence.

5. Corporations differ from proprietorships and partnerships in the following ways.

   a. Shareholders have limited liability.
   b. Ownership interests are easily transferred.
   c. They have the ability to raise large amounts of capital.
   d. They are separately taxed.
   e. They are often closely monitored and regulated by various government agencies.

6. Owners of a corporation are called stockholders (or shareholders), and those who operate a corporation are called managers. (Managers do not necessarily have to be shareholders; they are often hired by shareholders because of their managerial expertise.) A board of directors is annually elected by the shareholders to monitor management and govern the corporation.

7. Because the stocks of large corporations are traded daily on stock exchanges, shareholders can increase or decrease their ownership inter-

est in the firm by selling or buying shares of stock.

8. The two most typical types of stock are common and preferred. Common stock usually provides owners with voting rights (to elect directors and decide other matters), while preferred stock allows other privileges.

Accounting for Stock

9. Most stock has a par value, that is, a nominal value written on the face of each stock certificate. Although the par value does not relate to the issuance price of the stock (the price of most stocks is much higher than par value), it becomes the amount of legal capital of a business. This legal capital (number of shares outstanding times par value) is the minimum amount of owners' equity a company must maintain.

10. Stock that is issued at a price above par value is said to have been issued at a premium.

11. The entries to record the original issuance of stock are:

Par value stock:

Cash.................................   xxx
   Common (Preferred) Stock (par
     value × number of shares)   xxx
   Paid-In Capital in Excess of Par
     (excess cash received)   xxx

No-par stock:

Cash (amount received) ...   xxx
   Common (Preferred) Stock   xxx

These entries show that proceeds received from the issuance of stock are divided into the amount attributable to par value and the excess.

12. Stock that has been repurchased by a company is known as treasury stock. This stock is usually recorded at cost and is not separated into par value and excess paid. The entry to record the repurchase of treasury stock is:

Treasury Stock (cost)   xxx
   Cash   xxx

The account Treasury Stock is a contra-stockholders' equity account. Treasury stock is treated like unissued stock in that it possesses no voting, dividend, or other rights.

13. When treasury stock is reissued, it is credited at cost, and any excess of cash received over cost is credited to an account entitled Paid-In Capital, Treasury Stock. If the stock is sold for an amount less than cost, the Paid-In Capital,

Treasury Stock account is usually debited to the extent it exists, and excesses are debited to Retained Earnings.

14. The owners' equity section must show the different types of stock separately, the par value of the stocks, excess over par value, other paid-in capital sources, retained earnings, and treasury stock.

Retained Earnings

15. Retained Earnings is increased by earnings and decreased by losses and dividends. As pointed out in the Expanded Material, stockholders may receive a statement of retained earnings, which shows the beginning balance, additions and deductions, and the ending balance.

16. The distribution of corporate profits to shareholders is accomplished by paying dividends. Dividends can be paid in cash, other property, or additional shares of company stock.

17. The following three dates are important regarding dividends.

  a. *Declaration date*—date the dividend is declared payable by the board of directors. (This is the date a dividend becomes a liability.)

  b. *Record date*—date that identifies who will receive dividends.

  c. *Payment date*—date dividends are actually paid.

The entries to account for cash dividends are shown below.

Declaration Date:

Dividends   xxx
   Dividends Payable........   xxx

Record Date:
No entry.

Payment (Distribution) Date:

Dividends Payable............   xxx
   Cash...............................   xxx

18. The following types of dividend preferences can be associated with preferred stock.

  a. *Current-dividend preference*—the right to receive current dividends before common shareholders.

  b. *Cumulative-dividend preference*—the right to receive undistributed dividends from past years before the common shareholders receive any dividends for the current year.

The percentage usually associated with preferred stock indicates the amount of dividends preferred stockholders are to receive before common shareholders receive any dividends. This percentage multiplied by the number of outstanding shares at par value is their rightful share. The current-dividend preference allows this amount per year; the cumulative-dividend preference allows this amount for every year.

19. The dividend payout ratio tells financial statement users the percentage of the current year's net income that is paid out in the form of a cash dividend. It is computed by dividing cash dividends by net income.

Other Equity Items

20. The owners' equity section of a balance sheet can be separated into three parts: (a) contributed capital, which shows proceeds from the issuance of stock; (b) retained earnings, which discloses the undistributed cumulative earnings of a firm; and (c) comprehensive income, which summarizes the effect on equity that results from market-related increases and decreases in the reported values of assets and liabilities.

21. In recent years, a number of adjustments to the financial statements that were traditionally recorded as increases or decreases to income on the income statement are being made directly to the equity section of a balance sheet. Two of the most common "other equity" items reported in the comprehensive income section are (a) foreign currency translation adjustments, and (b) increases and decreases in the market value of available-for-sale securities (covered in Chapter 13).

22. Companies often include a statement of stockholders' equity in their annual reports, especially when significant changes have occurred in equity accounts other than retained earnings. This statement reconciles beginning and ending balances in all stockholders' equity accounts reported on the balance sheet, including retained earnings.

EXPANDED MATERIAL

Accounting for Stock Dividends

23. Additional shares of a company's stock may be distributed as a stock dividend instead of paying a cash dividend.

24. A stock dividend greater than 25 percent of total shares outstanding is considered to be a large stock dividend. When a large dividend is issued, Retained Earnings is debited for the par value

times the number of shares issued; when a small stock dividend is issued (less than 25 percent), Retained Earnings is debited for the market price times the number of shares issued. The rationale for this difference is that a large stock dividend will significantly reduce the market price of the stock, whereas a "small" dividend will not. The entries to account for the declaration and issuance of stock dividends are shown below.

Stock Dividend (small):
Retained Earnings xxx
    Common (Preferred) Stock   xxx
    Paid-In Capital in Excess of Par   xxx

Stock Dividend (large):
Retained Earnings xxx
    Common (Preferred) Stock   xxx

25. To encourage more investors to buy their stock, companies sometimes enact a stock split, replacing the existing shares with a larger number of new shares that sell at a lower price per share.

Prior-Period Adjustments

26. Prior-period adjustments are corrections and adjustments to the income of previous periods. Prior-period adjustments arise primarily when an error in one period is not caught until a subsequent period. Prior-period adjustments are made directly to the Retained Earnings account and therefore appear on a statement of retained earnings.

COMMON ERRORS

This chapter is usually quite easy for students. While there are no major concepts that present problems, the two most common errors are:

1. Failure to adjust the number of shares of stock when completing comprehensive stockholders' equity problems.

2. Recognizing a gain on the reissuance of treasury stock.

1. Adjusting the Number of Shares of Stock

A common type of homework problem in this chapter involves journalizing a series of stockholders' equity transactions and then preparing the stockholders' equity section of a balance sheet. Some journal entries involve issuing additional shares of either preferred or common stock, with a later entry involving the declaration of dividends. Since the dividends are usually declared and paid on a per-share basis, it is important to remember to update the number of shares of stock for each transaction.

The easiest way to eliminate this problem is to keep a running balance of the number of shares and the par values of preferred and common stock after each stockholders' equity transaction. This approach will also help you when you prepare the stockholders' equity section, since you will already know the correct numbers of shares of stock and par values, and you can check to see whether shares times par value equals the amount recorded in your stock accounts.

2. The Reissuance of Treasury Stock

You have just studied chapters on property, plant, and equipment and on long-term investments. In those chapters, when an asset was sold, any excess over book value was recognized as a gain. Now we tell you in this chapter that excess received over the cost of treasury stock is not a gain but additional paid-in capital. To avoid confusion over this apparent discrepancy, you should recognize that when a company reissues treasury stock, it is "selling" its own stock. When it sells an investment, it is selling stock or bonds of other corporations, and when it sells property, plant, and equipment, it is selling assets that have ready market values.

Companies cannot recognize gains when selling their own stock. If they could, they could easily manipulate earnings by buying their own stock and strategically selling it at a later date. And since companies have some control over their stock prices, gains could be recognized on nonindependent transactions—which violates the arm's-length transaction rule.

SELF-TEST

Matching

Instructions: Write the letter of each of the following terms in the space to the left of its appropriate definition.

a. cumulative-dividend preference
b. issued stock
c. common stock
d. comprehensive income
e. current-dividend preference
f. legal capital
g. contributed capital
h. stockholders
i. preferred stock

j. treasury stock
k. no-par stock
l. par value stock
m. prospectus
n. proprietorship
o. partnership
p. unlimited liability
q. prior-period adjustments
r. dividend payout ratio

_____ 1. The portion of owners' equity invested by owners through the issuance of stock.

_____ 2. The right of preferred shareholders to receive current dividends before common shareholders receive any dividends.

_____ 3. Stock that does not have a value assigned by the corporate charter and printed on the face of the stock certificate.

_____ 4. A type of income measurement that requires market-related gains and losses to be reported as separate equity items rather than included on the income statement.

_____ 5. A class of stock most frequently issued by corporations; it usually confers a voting right in the corporation; its dividend and liquidation rights are usually inferior to those of preferred stock.

_____ 6. The owners of a corporation.

_____ 7. The right of preferred shareholders to receive dividends for all past years in which no dividends were paid before common shareholders receive any dividends.

_____ 8. Authorized stock originally issued to stockholders, which may or may not still be outstanding.

_____ 9. A class of stock issued by corporations, usually having dividend and liquidation preferences over common stock.

_____ 10. Issued stock that has subsequently been reacquired and not retired by the corporation.

_____ 11. Stock that has a nominal value assigned to it in the corporation's charter and printed on the face of each share of stock.

_____ 12. The amount of contributed capital not available for dividends as restricted by state law for the protection of creditors.

_____ 13. The percentage of net income paid out during the year in the form of a cash dividend.

_____ 14. A report provided to potential investors that explains a company's business plan, sources of financing, and significant risks, and contains financial statements.

_____ 15. The absence of a ceiling on a proprietor's or partner's responsibility for the debts of the business.

_____ 16. An unincorporated business owned by one person.

_____ 17. An unincorporated business owned by two or more persons or entities.

EXPANDED MATERIAL

_____ 18. A category of events that restate net income from prior periods.

True/False

Instructions: Place a check mark in the appropriate column to indicate whether each of the following statements is true or false.

	True	False
1. Comprehensive income requires all market-related gains and losses to be reported on the income statement.	_____	_____
2. A corporation is a legal entity that is separate and distinct from its owners.	_____	_____
3. A disadvantage of a corporation is its unlimited liability.	_____	_____
4. The owners of a corporation are called shareholders, or stockholders.	_____	_____
5. Corporate income is not taxed separately from the income of the owners.	_____	_____
6. Stock that has been issued and bought back by a corporation is called outstanding stock.	_____	_____
7. When stock is issued at a price above par value, it is said to sell at a discount.	_____	_____
8. When no-par common stock is sold, Common Stock is credited for the total proceeds of the sale.	_____	_____
9. Treasury stock should be classified as an asset.	_____	_____
10. When treasury stock is purchased, it is typically recorded at cost.	_____	_____
11. The account Retained Earnings is never credited when accounting for treasury stock.	_____	_____
12. Dividends are the distribution of profits to shareholders.	_____	_____
13. The date that identifies who will receive a dividend is known as the declaration date.	_____	_____
14. Under the cumulative-dividend preference, preferred shareholders share any excess dividends equally with common shareholders.	_____	_____
15. The dividend payout ratio provides a measure of cash dividends paid as a percentage of total cash outflows for the period.	_____	_____

EXPANDED MATERIAL

	True	False
16. A stockholder owns a bigger percentage of a company after a stock dividend is received.	_____	_____
17. When "large" stock dividends are issued, Retained Earnings is debited at the par value of the stock.	_____	_____
18. Prior-period adjustments are made directly to the Retained Earnings account.	_____	_____
19. Corporations are required to present both a statement of retained earnings and a statement of stockholders' equity in their annual reports.	_____	_____

Multiple Choice

Instructions: Circle the letter that best completes each of the following statements.

1. Which of the following is *not* a feature of proprietorships and partnerships?
   a. Ease of formation
   b. Limited life
   c. Unlimited liability
   d. Separate taxation

2. Which of the following is *not* a feature of a corporation?
   a. Limited liability
   b. Easy transferability of ownership interests
   c. Separate taxation
   d. Unlimited liability

3. Stock that has been issued but not repurchased is called
   a. issued and outstanding stock.
   b. treasury stock.
   c. authorized but unissued stock.
   d. issued but not outstanding stock.

4. Excess paid-in capital would never be associated with
   a. no-par stock.
   b. par value stock.
   c. treasury stock.
   d. All of the above

5. Contributed capital that cannot be impaired is called
   a. paid-in capital.
   b. legal capital.
   c. stated capital.
   d. retained earnings.

6. Stock that is issued at a price above par is said to sell at
   a. a discount.
   b. a premium.
   c. stated value.
   d. par.

7. The entry for the issuance of common stock at par includes a
   a. credit to Cash.
   b. debit to Common Stock.
   c. credit to Common Stock.
   d. credit to Paid-In Capital.

8. Mammoth Company has 2,000 shares of $10 par value common stock outstanding. If it purchased 100 shares of its stock at $15, the entry would include a debit to Treasury Stock of
   a. $1,500.
   b. $1,000.
   c. Neither *a* nor *b*
   d. Either *a* or *b*

9. Treasury stock is

    a. an asset.
    b. a liability.
    c. a contra-stockholders' equity account.
    d. a revenue.

10. The account Paid-In Capital, Treasury Stock is credited when

    a. treasury stock is purchased at a price above par.
    b. treasury stock is sold at a price above cost.
    c. treasury stock is sold at a price below cost.
    d. treasury stock is purchased at a price below par.

11. The declaration and payment of a cash dividend

    a. increases Retained Earnings.
    b. decreases Retained Earnings.
    c. increases Contributed Capital.
    d. increases Cash.

12. The board of directors of a corporation first announces a dividend on the

    a. date of record.
    b. declaration date.
    c. payment date.
    d. dividend date.

13. The right of preferred shareholders to receive undistributed dividends from past years is called the

    a. current-dividend preference.
    b. cumulative-dividend preference.
    c. past year's preference.
    d. liquidation right.

14. A statement of stockholders' equity reports changes in

    a. contributed capital accounts.
    b. legal capital accounts.
    c. all stockholders' equity accounts.
    d. all balance sheet accounts.

EXPANDED MATERIAL

15. When a stock dividend is issued, total stockholders' equity

    a. increases.
    b. decreases.
    c. does not change.
    d. can be either increased or decreased.

16. Which of the following is *not* reported on a statement of retained earnings?

    a. Dividends declared and paid
    b. Net income
    c. Prior-period adjustments
    d. Comprehensive income

Exercises

E12-1   Issuance of Stock

Embarcadero Company was organized in 2006. During the first year of operations, it had the following stock transactions.

1. Issued 15,000 shares of $10 par value common stock to investors at $11.25 per share.

2. Issued 6,000 shares of $5 par value preferred stock to investors for $23 per share.

3. Issued 1,500 shares of no-par common stock for $8 per share.

4. Traded 4,000 shares of $5 par value preferred stock for a building. The market value of the building was $100,000.

Instructions: Prepare journal entries to record these transactions.

| | JOURNAL | | | PAGE | |
DATE	DESCRIPTION	POST. REF.	DEBIT	CREDIT

E12-2   Treasury Stock Transactions

Big John Company has 250,000 shares of $10 par value company stock outstanding. During 2006, the company had the following transactions.

1. January 15: Purchased 6,000 shares of its own stock at $20 per share.
2. February 2: Sold 1,500 shares of stock purchased in item 1 for $22 per share.
3. November 15: Sold 2,000 shares of stock purchased in item 1 for $18 per share.

Instructions: Prepare journal entries to record these transactions.

JOURNAL   PAGE

DATE	DESCRIPTION	POST. REF.	DEBIT	CREDIT

E12-3   Analysis of Stockholders' Equity

The stockholders' equity section of Green Bay Corporation at the end of 2006 showed the following.

Preferred stock (8%, $20 par, 15,000 shares authorized, 9,000 shares issued and outstanding)	$ X	
Common stock ($10 par value, 90,000 shares authorized, 60,000 issued, including 1,000 shares of treasury stock)	600,000	
Common stock (no-par, 9,000 shares authorized, 8,000 shares issued)	72,000	
Paid-in capital in excess of par value, preferred stock	X	
Paid-in capital in excess of par value, common stock	120,000	
Total contributed capital		$ X
Retained earnings		720,000
Less cost of treasury stock		(10,000)
Total stockholders' equity		$ X

Instructions: 1. What is the dollar amount in the Preferred Stock account?

2. What is the average price for which the $10 par value common stock was issued?

3. If the preferred stock was issued at an average price of $22 per share, what amount should appear in the Paid-In Capital in Excess of Par Value, Preferred Stock account?

4. What is the average cost per share of treasury stock?

5. Assuming that the $10 par value common stock and preferred stock were sold for average prices of $12 and $22, respectively, what is the total amount of contributed capital (including no-par common stock)?

6. Given the assumption in item 5, what is the total amount of stockholders' equity?

E12-4   Dividend Transactions

Ghiardelli Company had 20,000 shares of $10 par value common stock outstanding on January 1, 2006. The following dividend transactions occurred during the year.

Jan. 15:   Declared a $0.50-per-share cash dividend, payable on March 15 to shareholders of record on February 15.
Feb. 15:   Date of record.
Mar. 15:   Payment of cash dividend.

Instructions: Record the above transactions.

JOURNAL				PAGE	
DATE	DESCRIPTION	POST. REF.	DEBIT	CREDIT	

E12-5   Dividend Calculations

White Plains Corporation has the following stock outstanding:

  a. Common stock ($10 par, 10,000 shares outstanding)

  b. Preferred stock (6%, $5 par, 10,000 shares outstanding)

During the years 2004–2007, White Plains Corporation had net income of $20,000, $18,000, $5,000, and $30,000, respectively. The company has a policy of paying 50 percent of its income to shareholders as dividends, and no dividends are in arrears as of January 1, 2004.

Instructions: Compute the total amount of dividends that common and preferred shareholders would receive in each of the four years, assuming the following:
        1. The preferred stock is noncumulative.
        2. The preferred stock is cumulative.

E12-6   (Expanded material) Retained Earnings

Tonello Company was organized on January 1, 2004. On January 1, 2006, its Retained Earnings balance was $35,000. During 2006, it had the following:

Net income	$62,000
Dividends paid	41,000
Prior-period adjustment, reduction in inventory	17,000

Instructions: Use this information to prepare a retained earnings statement for 2006.

E12-7   (Expanded material) Stock Dividends and Stock Splits

The stockholders' equity section of Laura Jean Corporation's December 31, 2005, balance sheet included the following items:

Common stock ($1 par value, 20,000 shares issued and outstanding)..	$ 20,000	
Paid-in capital in excess of par value, common stock	120,000	
Total contributed capital		$140,000
Retained earnings...		240,000
Total stockholders' equity		$380,000

The following dividend transactions occurred during 2006:

Jun. 11:   A 2-for-1 stock split was declared.

Sep. 4:   A 15% stock dividend was declared and issued. The market price of the stock was $25 per share on the dividend date.

Instructions: Given this information, prepare journal entries to account for the above transactions.

JOURNAL   PAGE

DATE	DESCRIPTION	POST. REF.	DEBIT	CREDIT

ANSWERS

Matching

1.	g	7.	a	13.	r		
2.	e	8.	b	14.	m		
3.	k	9.	i	15.	p		
4.	d	10.	j	16.	n		
5.	c	11.	l	17.	o		
6.	h	12.	f	18.	q		

True/False

1.	F	8.	T	14.	F
2.	T	9.	F	15.	F
3.	F	10.	T	16.	F
4.	T	11.	T	17.	T
5.	F	12.	T	18.	T
6.	F	13.	F	19.	F
7.	F				

Multiple Choice

1.	d	7.	c	12.	b
2.	d	8.	a	13.	b
3.	a	9.	c	14.	c
4.	a	10.	b	15.	c
5.	b	11.	b	16.	d
6.	b				

Exercises

E12-1   Issuance of Stock

1. Cash.. 168,750
      Common Stock.. 150,000
      Paid-In Capital in Excess of Par Value, Common Stock............................ 18,750
   Issued 15,000 shares of $10 par value common stock at $11.25.

2. Cash.. 138,000
      Preferred Stock.. 30,000
      Paid-In Capital in Excess of Par Value, Preferred Stock 108,000
   Issued 6,000 shares of $5 par value preferred stock at $23.

3. Cash.. 12,000
      Common Stock.. 12,000
   Issued 1,500 shares of no-par common stock at $8.

4. Building.. 100,000
      Preferred Stock.. 20,000
      Paid-In Capital in Excess of Par Value, Preferred Stock............................ 80,000
   Issued 4,000 shares of $5 par value preferred stock for a building.

E12-2   Treasury Stock Transactions

1. January 15

Treasury Stock..	120,000	
Cash		120,000
Purchased 6,000 shares of treasury stock at $20 per share.		

2. February 2

Cash..	33,000	
Treasury Stock...		30,000
Paid-In Capital, Treasury Stock...		3,000
Resold 1,500 shares of treasury stock at $22 per share.		

3. November 15

Cash..	36,000	
Paid-In Capital, Treasury Stock...	3,000	
Retained Earnings...	1,000	
Treasury Stock..		40,000
Resold 2,000 shares of treasury stock at $18 per share.		

E12-3   Analysis of Stockholders' Equity

1. $180,000 (9,000 shares × $20).
2. $12 per share [($600,000 + $120,000)/60,000 shares].
3. $18,000 [($180,000 + X)/9,000 shares = $22].
4. $10 per share ($10,000/1,000 shares).
5. $990,000 ($180,000 + $600,000 + $72,000 + $18,000 + $120,000).
6. $1,700,000 ($990,000 + $720,000 – $10,000).

E12-4   Dividend Transactions

January 15

Dividends	10,000	
Dividends Payable..		10,000
Declared $0.50-per-share dividend on 20,000 shares.		

February 15   No entry

March 15

Dividends Payable..	10,000	
Cash..		10,000
Paid $0.50-per-share cash dividend.		

E12-5   Dividend Calculations

1. Preferred Stock—Noncumulative

Year	Common	Preferred	Total
2004	$ 7,000	$3,000	$10,000
2005	6,000	3,000	9,000
2006	—	2,500	2,500
2007	12,000	3,000	15,000

2. Preferred Stock—Cumulative

Year	Common	Preferred	Total
2004	$ 7,000	$3,000	$10,000
2005	6,000	3,000	9,000
2006	—	2,500	2,500
2007	11,500	3,500	15,000

Note: In this case, preferred stockholders get 6 percent every year, and since only $2,500 was paid in 2006, the $500 deficiency must be made up in 2007.

E12-6   (Expanded material) Retained Earnings

Tonello Company
Statement of Retained Earnings
For the Year Ended December 31, 2006

Retained earnings balance, January 1, 2006	$35,000
Prior-period adjustment: deduct adjustment for inventory correction	17,000
Balance as restated	$18,000
Net income for 2006	62,000
Total	$80,000
Less dividends declared and paid in 2006	41,000
Retained earnings balance, December 31, 2006	$39,000

E12-7   (Expanded material) Stock Dividends and Stock Splits

June 11

Retained Earnings	10,000	
Common Stock (10,000 × $1 par)		10,000

Declared a 2-for-1 stock split (20,000 × 0.50 = 10,000 shares).

September 4

Retained Earnings (4,500 shares × $25)	112,500	
Common Stock (4,500 × $1 par)		4,500
Paid-In Capital in Excess of Par, Common Stock		108,000

*Declared and issued a 15% common stock dividend
(30,000 × 0.15 = 4,500 shares).*

Chapter 13
Investments in Debt and Equity Securities

LEARNING OBJECTIVES

After studying this chapter, you should be able to:

1. Understand why companies invest in other companies.

2. Understand the different classifications for securities.

3. Account for the purchase, recognition of revenue, and sale of trading and available-for-sale securities.

4. Account for changes in the value of securities.

EXPANDED MATERIAL LEARNING OBJECTIVES

5. Account for held-to-maturity securities.

6. Account for securities using the equity method.

7. Understand the basics of consolidated financial statements.

CHAPTER REVIEW

Why Companies Invest in Other Companies

1. Firms often invest in other companies to earn a return through either interest/dividends or through increases in the value of the investment. Firms also invest in other companies to diversify their operations.

Classifying a Security

2. Firms can invest in both equity and debt securities. Debt securities are instruments issued by a company that carry a promise of repayment of interest and principal. Equity securities represent actual ownership in a corporation.

3. Investments in other companies are classified in four categories: (a) held-to-maturity, (b) equity method, (c) trading, and (d) available-for-sale.

   Held-to-maturity—Debt securities that are purchased with the intent of being held until maturity of the instrument. These investments are reported at amortized cost, and changes in fair value are not recorded on the financial statements.

   Equity method—Equity securities that represent ownership of 20 to 50 percent of the total stock outstanding of the investee. Equity method investments are recorded at cost, and adjusted for changes in the investee's net assets. Changes in fair value of the investment are not recorded on the financial statements.

Trading securities—Debt and equity securities purchased with the intent of being resold in the short run. Trading securities are recorded at fair value, and the change in value is reported on the income statement.

Available-for-sale—Debt and equity securities not classified as any of the above. These securities are recorded at fair value, but the change in value is not reported on the income statement; rather it is reported directly to equity.

Accounting for Trading and Available-for-Sale Securities

4. All investments, regardless of their classification, are initially recorded at their cost. This cost includes the price of the security plus any additional related expenditures. The most common additional expenditure is broker's fees.

5. Furthermore, debt securities (as explained in Chapter 10) are usually sold at a premium or a discount (the difference between purchase price and face value). This premium or discount only affects held-to-maturity securities.

6. As noted, both trading securities and available-for-sale securities are reported at fair value. Therefore the accounting treatment is similar for these two categories.

7. The amount of cash received by an investor is recorded as dividend or revenue income on the income statement.

8. Gains or losses resulting from the sale of an investment are recorded as income on the income statement. A gain or loss is the difference between the book value of the investment and the proceeds of the sale. For example, if Company A sells equity securities for $10,000 and the value of the securities on the accounting records is $9,000, the recorded gain on the sale would be $1,000.

Accounting for Changes in the Value of Securities

9. The changes in value of a trading security are recorded as income even though the security has not been sold. For example, a trading security purchased at $1,000 is now worth $1,200. This increase in value of the trading security would be recorded as follows:

Market-Adjustment—
Trading Securities 200
   Unrealized Gain on Trading
     Securities—Income 200

The market adjustment account is an asset account if it has a debit balance or a contra-asset account if it has a credit balance.

10. Changes in value of available-for-sale securities are not recorded as income but are rather an adjustment made directly to equity.

11. The market adjustment account is a balance sheet account. Therefore, if the value changes again, the account is adjusted to the new balance. For example, if the securities in item 9 were subsequently worth $900, the needed adjustment would be $300 since the balance in the market adjustment account is now $200 debit and it should have a $100 credit balance. The entry would be as follows:

Unrealized Loss on Trading
Securities—Income 300
   Market-Adjustment—
     Trading Securities 300

EXPANDED MATERIAL

Accounting for Held-to-Maturity Securities

12. Only debt securities can be classified as held-to-maturity. Bonds are the most common type of held-to-maturity security.

13. When bonds are acquired, the investment is recorded at cost. If bonds are purchased between interest payment dates, investors must pay for any interest accrued since the last payment date. The accrued interest advanced to sellers is debited to Bond Interest Receivable. When the next interest payment is received, a credit is made to both Bond Interest Receivable and Bond Interest Revenue in order to reflect the net interest actually earned.

14. When interest is received on bond investments, Bond Interest Revenue is credited and Cash is debited.

15. When bonds are purchased at amounts either below or above face value, the difference (discount or premium) must be written off (amortized) over the life of the bonds. For example, if a 10-year, $10,000 bond is sold for $11,000, the premium of $1,000 must be amortized over the 10 years, so that at maturity the investment will be shown at only $10,000—the amount to be repaid to investors. Although there are several ways to amortize premiums and discounts, the easiest is the straight-line method, which in this example would result in an amortization of $100 per year ($1,000/10 years). The amortiza-

tion of a premium results in a decrease in interest revenue, while the amortization of a discount results in an increase in interest revenue. Finally, the amortization entries can be combined with the periodic interest entries explained in item 14.

16. If bonds are held to maturity, investors simply receive the face amount of the bonds. If, however, they sell the bonds before maturity, they can have a gain or loss, depending on the price at which the bonds are sold. If the bonds are sold for more than their carrying value, a gain is realized; if sold for less, a loss results.

17. Although the straight-line method of amortization is easiest and often can be justified, another method, known as effective-interest amortization, is theoretically more appropriate. This method computes the amount of amortization by multiplying the effective interest rate by the investment balance to arrive at the actual interest earned; computing the difference between the interest earned and the interest received to get the amortization amount; and then either adding or subtracting the amortization to the investment balance to arrive at a new bond carrying amount. Because effective-interest amortization considers both the actual interest earned and the changing balance of the investment, it is the preferred method.

Accounting for Equity Investments Using the Equity Method

18. A company may purchase the stock of another company for several reasons. Management may feel that the investment will earn a good return; they may like the regularity of the dividends paid on the stock; or they may want to gain control of another company. A company that owns and controls another company is called a parent company; the company owned is called a subsidiary.

19. When 20–50 percent of a company is owned, the investment usually is accounted for on the equity basis.

20. The entries to account for investments carried on the equity basis are different from other investment entries. While investments are recorded at cost when purchased, they are decreased when dividends are received and increased when the subsidiary recognizes periodic earnings.

Consolidated Financial Statements

21. If an investor is able to control the decisions made by the investee, the investor should prepare consolidated financial statements. Generally when an investor owns over 50 percent of the voting stock of an investee, the investor is presumed to control the decisions made by the investee.

22. The purpose of consolidation is to create financial statement for the parent and its controlled subsidiaries to report their performance as if they were one company.

23. To consolidate, the parent company adds all the assets, liabilities, revenues, and expenses of the controlled subsidiaries to its own financial statements. When accounting for those subsidiaries that are less than 100 percent owned, the parent company must reduce the financial statements by the percentage of the subsidiary that is not owned by the parent company. The percentage not owned by the parent is called the minority interest. The amount subtracted from the liabilities and equity side of the balance sheet is known as "Minority interest," and the amount subtracted from the income statement is known as "Minority interest income."

COMMON ERRORS

The problems students have with the material in this chapter are different for each method of accounting for long-term investments.

1. **Trading and Available-for-Sale Securities**

   In accounting for trading and available-for-sale securities, the most common errors made relate to adjusting securities to their market values. Remember that held-to-maturity securities and equity method securities are not adjusted for temporary changes in market value. For trading and available-for-sale securities, securities are adjusted to their fair values using a market adjustment account. The difference between the two types of securities relates to the offset to the market adjustment account. For trading securities, the offset goes through the income statement. For available-for-sale securities, the offset to market adjustment is to a stockholders' equity account.

2. **Held-to-Maturity Securities (Expanded material)**

   In accounting for held-to-maturity securities, the most common errors are:

a. Confusing the accounting for premiums and discounts on long-term investments with the accounting required for bonds payable.

When a company makes a long-term investment in bonds, it does not record the premium or discount separately. Remember that all assets are initially recorded at cost, which is not the case with payables, as you learned in Chapter 10 (where the premium or discount was recorded separately). For example, if a long-term bond is purchased at 102 1/2 on an interest date, the premium should be included in the Investment account, not in a separate account. Thus, this investment should be recorded at $102,500, not $100,000. Following are the correct and incorrect entries to record this investment.

Correct:

Investment	102,500	
Cash		102,500

Incorrect:

Investment	100,000	
Premium	2,500	
Cash		102,500

b. Failing to amortize the premium or discount.

Since the premium or discount has been included in the Investment account, students tend to forget that they must amortize that amount. If it is not amortized, at the end of the investment period the Investment account will not show the proper face value, and the premium or discount will not have been included as part of the annual interest revenue. Referring again to the $102,500 investment in bonds, assume that the bonds are due to mature in 5 years and that the stated rate of interest is 10 percent. The following entry would be made every 6 months when the investing company receives the interest (assuming the straight-line method of amortization).

Cash.....................................	5,000	
Investment		250
Bond Interest Revenue ...		4,750

To record the collection of interest and to amortize the bond premium ($2,500 ÷ 10 periods = $250).

Following this procedure, the Investment account will be at $100,000 on the maturity date of the bonds, when the company is entitled to collect $100,000 from the issuing company.

3. The Equity Method (Expanded material)

When the equity method is used, we assume that the investing company owns 20 to 50 percent of the investee company's stock. This means that increases and decreases in the investee company's equity accounts should be properly accounted for by the investing company. Students frequently forget to increase such long-term investments for the company's share of the investee company's earnings and to decrease the investment for dividends received. Remember, earnings reflect an increase in the value of the investment. Dividends paid to the investing company represent a decrease in the investment; otherwise, the amount of the dividends would be accounted for twice, as part of the investment and as a return on the investment. At the end of an accounting period, the Investment account should include the following elements.

Original cost of the investment	xxx
+ Investor's share of all the earnings since the original investment	xx
− All cash dividends received from the investee since the original investment	(xx)
Balance of investment at equity for the current balance sheet	xxx

To accomplish this, you must make a journal entry when dividends are received and, at year-end, an adjusting entry to increase the Investment account for the investor's share of the investee's earnings.

SELF-TEST

Matching

Instructions: Write the letter of each of the following terms in the space to the left of its appropriate definition.

a.	bond discount	**g.**	market adjustment
b.	bond premium	**h.**	effective-interest amortization
c.	trading securities	**i.**	amortization
d.	available-for-sale securities	**j.**	straight-line amortization
e.	held-to-maturity securities	**k.**	equity method
f.	consolidation	**l.**	minority interest

_____ 1. The difference between the face value and the sales price of a bond when it is purchased below its face value.

_____ 2. The difference between the face value and the sales price of a bond when it is purchased above its face value.

_____ 3. Securities purchased with the intent of holding the securities until they mature.

_____ 4. Debt and equity method securities purchased with the intent of selling them should the need for cash arise or to realize short-term gains.

_____ 5. Debt and equity securities not classified as trading, held-to-maturity, or equity method securities.

_____ 6. An account used to track the difference between the historical cost and the market value of a company's portfolio of trading and available-for-sale securities.

EXPANDED MATERIAL

_____ 7. A method of systematically writing off a bond premium or discount that takes into consideration the time value of money; results in an equal interest rate for each period.

_____ 8. The systematic writing off of a bond discount or premium over the life of the bond.

_____ 9. Accounting for an investment in another company where significant influence can be imposed by recording the initial acquisition at cost but recognizing dividends as return of investments and the proportionate share of earnings as revenue.

_____ 10. Accounting for an investment in one or more companies where the parent company controls the decisions made by the other company or companies.

_____ 11. A method of systematically writing off a bond premium or discount in equal amounts each period until maturity.

_____ 12. The amount of equity investment made by outside shareholders to consolidated subsidiaries that are not 100% owned by the parent.

True/False

Instructions: Place a check mark in the appropriate column to indicate whether each of the following statements is true or false.

	True	False
1. In accounting for an investment as a trading or available-for-sale security, the entry to record the receipt of dividends includes a credit to the Investment account.	_____	_____
2. Trading securities are not recorded at fair value.	_____	_____
3. When investments in debt securities are sold before maturity at amounts greater than their carrying value, a gain is realized.	_____	_____
4. Securities that are held with the intent of selling them should the need for cash arise are properly classified as available-for-sale securities.	_____	_____
5. The account Market Adjustment—Trading Securities is disclosed on the balance sheet.	_____	_____
6. Held-to-maturity securities can include both debt and equity investments.	_____	_____

	True	False
7. All investments in debt and equity securities are valued at their market value.	_____	_____
8. Unrealized gains and losses result from changes in the price of securities while the security is still being held.	_____	_____

EXPANDED MATERIAL

9. When a company owns between 20 and 50 percent of the outstanding voting stock of another company, it must usually account for that investment on the equity basis.   _____   _____

10. Investments that are accounted for on the equity basis are not valued at fair value. ....   _____   _____

11. When a held-to-maturity investment is sold, the calculation of the gain or loss includes a consideration of that stock's share of the existing Market Adjustment—Held-to-Maturity Securities. ....   _____   _____

12. Investors who want to earn an interest rate that is higher than the stated rate will pay a premium for held-to-maturity securities. ....   _____   _____

13. When held-to-maturity securities are purchased between interest payment dates, the investor must pay for any accrued interest from the last interest payment date to the date of purchase. ....   _____   _____

14. Present value concepts are used to determine how much to pay for held-to-maturity securities. ....   _____   _____

15. When a held-to-maturity security is purchased as a long-term investment, the face value of the security is recorded in the Investment account and any premium or discount is recorded separately. ....   _____   _____

16. Theoretically, the most correct way to amortize bond premiums or discounts is the straight-line method. ....   _____   _____

17. The amortization of a premium increases the amount of interest earned on an investment. ....   _____   _____

18. Interest revenue, when computed using the effective-interest amortization method, is equal to the investment balance times the stated interest rate of the bonds. ....   _____   _____

19. The entry to amortize a bond discount or premium is made directly to the Investment account, which results in an increase or a decrease in that balance. ....   _____   _____

20. When a company owns over 50 percent of the outstanding voting stock of another company, it must usually consolidate the financial statements of that company with its own financial statements. ....   _____   _____

21. For companies that consolidate, the minority interest accounts are optional when the company owns less than 100 percent of the subsidiary. ....   _____   _____

Multiple Choice

Instructions: Circle the letter that best completes each of the following statements.

1. Which of the following investments is *not* valued at fair market value?

   a. Long-term investments in the stock of another company (up to 20 percent ownership)
   b. Long-term investments in the stock of another company (more than 20 percent ownership)
   c. Short-term investments in the stock of another company
   d. Short-term investments in bonds

2. Trading securities are valued at fair value

   a. on an individual asset basis.
   b. on a portfolio basis.
   c. never.
   d. only if they are investments in bonds.

3. When an investment in stock is considered available-for-sale, the entry to record the receipt of a dividend includes a

   a. credit to Dividend Revenue.
   b. credit to Investment in Stock.
   c. credit to Cash.
   d. debit to Investment in Stock.

4. The account Market Adjustment is credited when which of the following types of investments is reduced to market value?

   a. Held-to-maturity securities
   b. Investments in stocks accounted for on the equity basis
   c. Trading securities
   d. None of the above

5. Which of the following is a stockholders' equity account?

   a. Unrealized Decrease in Value of Available-for-Sale Securities
   b. Market Adjustment—Available-for-Sale Securities
   c. Unrealized Loss on Trading Securities
   d. Realized Gain on Sale of Securities

6. Held-to-maturity securities are carried at

   a. adjusted cost.
   b. equity.
   c. lower of cost or market.
   d. None of the above

7. Available-for-sale securities are securities that are

   a. purchased with the intent of selling them should the need for cash arise.
   b. purchased with the intent of holding them until they mature.
   c. purchased with the intent of taking advantage of short-term increases in price.
   d. not classified as trading, held-to-maturity, or equity method securities.

8. The account Market Adjustment—Trading Securities is

   a. a stockholders' equity account.
   b. a nominal account that contains the current period's increase or decrease in value of trading securities.
   c. an account that adjusts trading securities from cost to market.
   d. a balance sheet account that tracks the change in value of the trading securities for the current period.

EXPANDED MATERIAL

9. Which of the following is *not* a characteristic of a held-to-maturity security?

   a. It often can be sold for cash.
   b. Management plans to sell the asset within the current year.
   c. It may be an investment in the bonds of another company.
   d. It is not usually a temporary investment of excess cash.

10. When a company owns 30 percent of the outstanding voting stock of another company, that investment generally should be accounted for on

    a. the equity basis.
    b. the cost basis.
    c. an account that adjusts trading securities from cost to market.
    d. a balance sheet account that tracks the change in value of the trading securities for the current period.

11. When an investment in stock is accounted for on the equity basis, the entry to record a receipt of dividends includes a

    a. credit to Dividend Revenue.
    b. credit to Investment in Stock.
    c. credit to Cash.
    d. debit to Dividend Revenue.

12. The market price of a held-to-maturity security is a function of which of the following?

    a. The stability of the organization issuing the security
    b. The interest rate at which the securities are issued
    c. Both *a* and *b*
    d. Neither *a* nor *b*

13. If an investor wants to earn 12 percent on an investment, how much should he or she pay to buy $60,000 of 20-year bonds with a stated interest rate of 10 percent (interest paid annually)?

    a. $60,000
    b. $51,038
    c. $44,816
    d. $62,200

14. Premiums and discounts must be amortized over the bond's

    a. outstanding period.
    b. legal life.
    c. Either *a* or *b*
    d. Neither *a* nor *b*

15. When the effective-interest amortization method is used, interest revenue is equal to the

    a. investment balance times the stated rate of interest.
    b. face value of the bonds times the stated rate of interest.
    c. face value of the bonds times the effective rate of interest.
    d. investment balance times the effective rate of interest.

16. When a company owns over 50 percent of the outstanding voting stock of another company, that investment generally should be accounted for using

    a. the equity method
    b. the cost method
    c. the consolidation method
    d. an account that adjusts trading securities from cost to market

17. When a consolidated subsidiary is less than 100 percent owned by the parent company, the accounts that represent the amounts owned by outside investors are known as

    a. minority interest
    b. disowned securities
    c. residual interest
    d. hidden interest

Exercises

E13-1   Investments in Stock (No Significant Influence Exercised)

The following transactions relate to the investment activities of Jordan Company during 2006 and 2007.

1. (2006) Purchased as an available-for-sale security 800 shares of Dog Corporation stock at $22 per share plus $400 brokerage fees.

2. (2006) Purchased as a trading security 500 shares of RST Corporation stock at $20 per share plus $200 brokerage fees.

3. (2006) Received a $3-per-share dividend on the Dog Corporation stock.

4. (2006) The market values of the stocks on the last day of the year were:

    a. Dog Corporation stock: $24 per share
    b. RST Corporation stock: $16 per share

5. (2007) Sold all 800 shares of Dog Corporation stock at $25 per share.

Instructions: Journalize these transactions.

JOURNAL   PAGE

DATE	DESCRIPTION	POST. REF.	DEBIT	CREDIT

E13-2   (Expanded material) Long-Term Investments in Stocks

During 2006, Leonard Company made two long-term investments. It purchased from R-2 Company 2,000 of a total 12,000 shares outstanding; it purchased from J-1 Company 3,000 of a total 10,000 shares outstanding. Leonard Company paid $12 per share for the R-2 stock and $50 per share for the J-1 stock. During 2006, Leonard received dividends of $1 and $3 per share on the stocks, respectively. On December 31, 2006, total reported earnings and per share market prices for the companies were as follows:

	R-2 Company	J-1 Company
Earnings	$30,000	$50,000
Per share market prices	11	48

Instructions: Record journal entries to account for (1) the investments, (2) the dividends received, (3) recognition of investee company earnings, and (4) adjustment to market. (You may omit explanations for the journal entries.)

JOURNAL   PAGE

DATE	DESCRIPTION	POST. REF.	DEBIT	CREDIT

E13-3   (Expanded material) Present Value of Held-to-Maturity Securities

Able Company is offering $10,000 of 8 percent bonds for sale. The bonds mature in 20 years and pay interest every 6 months.

Instructions: How much would you pay for the bonds if you wanted to earn 16 percent on your investment?

E13-4   (Expanded material) Long-Term Investments in Held-to-Maturity Securities

On September 1, 2005, Raymond Corporation purchased $100,000 of Chester Company's 6 percent, 10-year bonds at 94.4. The bonds were dated January 1, 2005, and pay interest semiannually on June 30 and December 31.

Instructions: Give the required entries to account for Raymond's investment in these bonds on each of the following dates. (Raymond uses the straight-line method and amortizes the discount as part of each interest-payment-received entry.)
1. September 1, 2005.
2. December 31, 2005.
3. June 30, 2006.
4. December 31, 2006.

	JOURNAL			PAGE
DATE	DESCRIPTION	POST. REF.	DEBIT	CREDIT

E13-5   (Expanded material) Consolidated Financial Statements

Parent Company owns parts of three different subsidiaries. The balance sheet and income statements for these four companies are listed below. Note that, in the financial statements of Parent Company, its ownership interest in the three subsidiaries has been accounted for using the equity method.

| | | Percentage of the Parent's Ownership | | |
| | | 100% | 70% | 40% |
	Parent	**Sub 1**	**Sub 2**	**Sub 3**
Assets				
Cash	$ 65	$ 20	$ 30	$ 40
Accounts receivable	250	80	90	40
Plant and equipment	750	300	400	200
Investment in Sub 1	200			
Investment in Sub 2	154			
Investment in Sub 3	48			
Total assets	$1,467	$400	$520	$280
Liabilities	850	200	300	160
Equity	617	200	220	120
Total liabilities and equity	$1,467	$400	$520	$280
Sales	5,340	3,000	3,000	2,000
Income from Sub 1	300			
Income from Sub 2	140			
Income from Sub 3	40			
Expenses	(3,500)	(2,700)	(2,800)	(1,900)
Net income	$2,320	$ 300	$ 200	$ 100

Instructions: Prepare both (1) a consolidated balance sheet and (2) a consolidated income statement for Parent Company and its subsidiaries.

ANSWERS

Matching

1.	a	5.	d	9.	k
2.	b	6.	g	10.	f
3.	e	7.	h	11.	j
4.	c	8.	i	12.	l

True/False

1.	F	8.	T	15.	F
2.	F	9.	T	16.	F
3.	T	10.	T	17.	F
4.	F	11.	F	18.	F
5.	T	12.	F	19.	T
6.	F	13.	T	20.	T
7.	F	14.	T	21.	F

Multiple Choice

1.	b	7.	d	13.	b
2.	b	8.	c	14.	a
3.	a	9.	b	15.	d
4.	c	10.	a	16.	c
5.	a	11.	b	17.	a
6.	a	12.	c		

Exercises

E13-1   Investments in Stock (No Significant Influence Exercised)

1. Investment in Available-for-Sale Securities, Dog Corporation Stock............. 18,000
      Cash... 18,000
    Purchased 800 shares of Dog Corporation stock at $22 per share plus $400 brokerage fees.

2. Investment in Trading Securities, RST Corporation Stock 10,200
      Cash... 10,200
    Purchased 500 shares of RST Corporation stock at $20 per share plus $200 brokerage fees.

3. Cash... 2,400
      Dividend Revenue 2,400
    Received a $3-per-share dividend on 800 shares of Dog Corporation stock.

4. a.   Market Adjustment—Available-for-Sale Securities 1,200
            Unrealized Increase in Value of Available-for-Sale Securities—Equity 1,200
    b.   Unrealized Loss on Trading Securities—Income 2,200
            Market Adjustment—Trading Securities 2,200

5. Cash... 20,000
      Investment in Available-for-Sale Securities, Dog Corporation Stock......... 18,000
      Gain on Sale of Investment in Available-for-Sale Securities...................... 2,000
    Sold 800 shares of Dog Corporation stock at $25 per share.

E13-2   (Expanded material) Long-Term Investments in Stocks

R-2 Company

Method of accounting   Available-for-Sale (16.6% ownership)

1. Investment entries

Investment in Available-for-Sale Securities, R-2 Company	24,000	
Cash..		24,000

2. Receipt of dividends

Cash..	2,000	
Dividend Revenue		2,000

3. Recognition of subsidiary's earnings
No entry

4. Adjustment to market value

Unrealized Decrease in Value of Available-for-Sale Securities—Equity	2,000	
Market Adjustment—Available-for-Sale Securities...................................		2,000

J-1 Company

Method of accounting   Equity (30% ownership)

1. Investment entries

Investment in Equity Method Securities, J-1 Company Stock	150,000	
Cash..		150,000

2. Receipt of dividends

Cash..	9,000	
Investment in Equity Method Securities, J-1 Company Stock		9,000

3. Recognition of subsidiary's earnings

Investment in Equity Method Securities, J-1 Company Stock	15,000	
Revenue from Investments (30% of $50,000)...		15,000

4. Adjustment to market value
No entry—equity method

E13-3   (Expanded material) Present Value of Held-to-Maturity Securities

$10,000			$400	Semiannual interest payment
0.0460	(Table I)		11.9246	Present value of an annuity factor: 8% for 40 periods (Table II)
$460			$4,769.84	

Sum
$5,229.84

E13-4   (Expanded material) Long-Term Investments in Held-to-Maturity Securities

1. September 1, 2005

Investment in Held-to-Maturity Securities, Chester Company	94,400	
Bond Interest Receivable	1,000	
Cash..		95,400

Invested in Chester Company bonds.

Bond investment: $100,000 at 94.4 = $94,400. Accrued interest: $100,000 × 0.06 × 2/12 = $1,000.

2. December 31, 2005

Investment in Held-to-Maturity Securities, Chester Company	200	
Cash..	3,000	
Bond Interest Receivable		1,000
Bond Interest Revenue		2,200

To record the receipt of semiannual interest on Chester Company bonds and to record the investment amortization.

Amortization: ($100,000 − $94,400) ÷ 112 months = $50 per month × 4 months = $200.
Cash received: $100,000 × 0.06 × 1/2 = $3,000.
Interest revenue: $3,000 + $200 − $1,000 = $2,200.

3. June 30, 2006

Investment in Held-to-Maturity Securities, Chester Company	300	
Cash..	3,000	
Bond Interest Revenue		3,300

To record the receipt of semiannual interest on Chester Company bonds and to record the investment amortization.

Amortization: $50 × 6 months = $300.

4. December 31, 2006
This entry is the same as for June 30, 2006.

E13-5 (Expanded material) Consolidated Financial Statements

1.

Parent Company and Subsidiaries
Consolidated Balance Sheet

Assets	
Cash ($65 + $20 + $30)	$ 115
Accounts receivable ($250 + $80 + $90)...	420
Plant and equipment ($750 + $300 + $400)..	1,450
Investment in Sub 3 ($120 × 0.40)	48
Total assets	$ 2,033
Liabilities ($850 + $200 + $300)	1,350
Minority interest ($220 × 0.30)...	66
Equity...	617
Total liabilities and equity	$ 2,033

2.

Parent Company and Subsidiaries
Consolidated Income Statement

Revenues	
Sales ($5,340 + $3,000 + $3,000)..	$ 11,340
Income from Sub 3 ($100 × 0.40)..	40
Expenses ($3,500 + $2,700 + $2,800)..	(9,000)
Minority interest income ($200 × 0.30)..	(60)
Net income..	$ 2,320

Chapter 14
Statement of Cash Flows

LEARNING OBJECTIVES

After studying this chapter, you should be able to:

1. Understand the purpose of a statement of cash flows.

2. Recognize the different types of information reported in the statement of cash flows.

3. Prepare a simple statement of cash flows.

4. Analyze financial statements to prepare a statement of cash flows.

5. Use information from the statement of cash flows to make decisions.

CHAPTER REVIEW

What Is the Purpose of a Statement of Cash Flows?

1. The primary purpose of the statement of cash flows is to provide information about the cash receipts and payments of an entity during a period of time. This information can be used to evaluate a company's ability to generate positive net cash flows in the future to meet its obligations and to pay dividends.

2. A statement of cash flows also explains the changes in the balance sheet accounts and the cash effects of the accrual-basis amounts reported in the income statement. The cash flow statement complements the balance sheet and income statement and is one of the three primary financial statements.

What Information Is Reported in the Statement of Cash Flows?

3. When preparing a statement of cash flows, cash should include cash equivalents, which are short-term, highly liquid investments (Treasury bills, money market funds, and commercial paper) that can be easily converted to cash.

4. On a statement of cash flows, the inflows and outflows of cash must be classified into three main categories: operating activities, investing activities, and financing activities.

5. Operating activities include all cash flows that enter into the determination of net income. Major operating cash inflows are cash receipts from sales and other cash revenues; major operating cash outflows are cash payments to purchase inventory and pay operating expenses.

Dividend receipts and interest receipts and payments are included in operating activities.

6. Investing activities include cash outflows to purchase stocks and bonds of other companies (except cash equivalents) not classified as trading securities; property, plant, and equipment, and other assets to be used in the business; and the making and collecting of loans. Investing activities also include cash inflows from the sale of these same investments.

7. Financing activities include transactions and events where resources are obtained from or repaid to owners (equity financing) and creditors (debt financing). The payment of dividends and the purchase of treasury stock are financing activities.

8. The format of the statement of cash flows should provide a reconciliation of the beginning and ending balances of cash (and cash equivalents).

9. Noncash investing and financing transactions, such as purchasing land by issuing stock or paying off long-term debt by issuing stock, are not shown in the statement of cash flows but are reported in a note or in a separate schedule.

Preparing a Statement of Cash Flows—A Simple Example

10. If detailed cash flow information is readily available from the cash account, the preparation of a statement of cash flows is straightforward. The cash inflows and outflows merely need to be classified according to type of activity—operating, investing, and financing.

11. By properly coding information when input into a computerized accounting system, accounting software can make the preparation of a cash flow statement very easy.

Analyzing the Other Primary Financial Statements to Prepare a Statement of Cash Flows

12. If detailed cash flow information is not readily available, a statement of cash flows can be prepared by analyzing the income statement and comparative balance sheets.

13. By analyzing the change in balance sheet accounts in relation to income statement data, cash flows for the period can be determined. For example, the beginning accounts receivable balance plus sales for the period less the ending accounts receivable balance equals the amount of cash collected from customers, which would be reported as an operating item on the statement of cash flows. A similar analysis is required for each balance sheet account and related income statement amounts.

14. A six-step process can be used in preparing a statement of cash flows, as follows:

a. Compute the change in the cash and cash-equivalent accounts for the period of the statement. This is a check figure.

b. Convert income statement amounts from an accrual-basis to a cash-basis summary of operations. This is done by (a) eliminating any income statement expenses that do not involve cash (e.g., depreciation); (b) eliminating any effects of non-operating activities (e.g., gain or loss on sale of equipment); and (c) adjusting current asset and liability operating accounts (other than cash) to a cash basis.

c. Analyze long-term assets to identify the cash flow effects of investing activities.

d. Analyze long-term debt and stockholders' equity accounts to determine cash flow effects of financing activities.

e. Prepare a formal statement of cash flows by classifying all cash inflows and outflows according to operating, investing, and financing activities. The net cash flow for the period should be the same amount computed in the first step (a). The net increase (decrease) in cash for the period is then added (subtracted) to the beginning cash balance to reconcile to the ending cash balance.

f. Report any significant noncash investing or financing transactions (e.g., purchasing land by issuing stock) in a narrative explanation or on a separate schedule to the statement of cash flows.

15. The statement of cash flows can be prepared using either the direct or the indirect method. The difference between the two methods is in the way the cash flows from operating activities are presented; the format for presenting cash flows from investing and financing activities is the same for both methods.

16. The indirect method involves a reconciliation between net income and net cash flows from operations. With the indirect method, net income is adjusted for items that do not affect cash, such as depreciation, and for differences between reported (accrual) revenues and expenses and cash received and spent for those revenues and expenses. The indirect method is

favored by most accountants and companies because it is easier to prepare.

17. When using the indirect method, net cash received (paid) from operating activities is determined by adjusting accrual-based net income to cash received from (paid for) operations. When adjusting net income, decreases in receivables and other current operating assets, increases in payables and other current operating liabilities, and noncash expenses, such as depreciation, are added to net income; increases in current operating assets and decreases in current operating liabilities are deducted from net income. This calculation is shown below (with arbitrary numbers).

Cash Flows from Operating Activities:

Net income $60,400

Add (deduct) adjustments to cash basis:

Increase in accounts receivable	(8,000)
Decrease in interest receivable	2,000
Decrease in inventory......................	18,000
Decrease in prepaid insurance.........	2,400
Increase in accounts payable	5,500
Increase in wages payable	2,000
Decrease in interest payable	(3,000)
Decrease in taxes payable	(5,000)
Depreciation	12,000
Net cash flow provided by (used in) operating activities	$86,300

18. Increases in receivables and other current operating assets are subtracted from net income because less cash was received (some of it is still owed and will be collected next period) than was reported as a revenue; increases in payables are added to net income because they have not yet been paid, and thus less cash was spent than was reported as an expense on the income statement. The opposite logic explains why decreases in receivables and other assets are added and why decreases in payables are subtracted. Depreciation and other noncash expenses are added because even though they decreased net income, they did not require any cash. Adjustments must also be made for gains and losses on the sale of assets.

19. The direct method shows separately the major classes of operating cash receipts, such as cash collected from customers and cash received from interest or dividends, and cash payments, such as cash paid to suppliers for goods and services, to creditors for interest, and to the government for taxes. With the direct method, the difference between operating cash receipts and cash payments is the net cash flow pro-

vided by (used in) operations. The direct method is favored by many user groups because it is straightforward and is not likely to be misunderstood.

20. Accrual-based revenues can be converted to cash received by adding the appropriate beginning receivable balances and subtracting the ending receivable balances as follows (with arbitrary numbers):

Income statement amount (sales, interest revenue, or dividend revenue)............................	$300,000
+ Beginning receivable amount (accounts receivable, interest receivable, or dividend receivable) .	12,000
− Ending receivable amount (accounts receivable, interest receivable, or dividend receivable) .	(8,000)
= Cash collected from revenue (sales, interest, or dividends)...........	$304,000

21. Cost of goods sold can be converted to cash paid for inventory by first determining purchases for the period and then determining the amount of cash paid for purchases during the period as follows (with arbitrary numbers):

Determining Purchases:

Cost of goods sold	$200,000
+ Ending inventory	15,000
− Beginning inventory	(18,000)
= Purchases during the period........	$197,000

Determining Cash Paid for Purchases:

Purchases during the period........	$197,000
+ Beginning accounts payable	22,000
− Ending accounts payable	(15,000)
= Cash paid for inventory	$204,000

22. Cash paid for expenses such as wages, rent, insurance, and taxes can be determined by adding appropriate beginning payables and ending prepaid balances and subtracting ending payables and beginning prepaid balances, as shown below (with arbitrary numbers).

Reported expenses (wages, insurance, taxes, etc.)	$100,000
+ Beginning payable balance (wages payable, etc.)	5,000
+ Ending prepaid balance (prepaid wages, etc.)...................	0
− Ending payable balance (wages payable, etc.)	(4,000)
− Beginning prepaid balance (prepaid wages, etc.)...................	0
= Cash paid for expenses	$101,000

Obviously, some expenses will have balances in the prepaid accounts, while some will have balances in the liability accounts. Only on rare occasions will there be balances in both for the same expenses.

23. When using the direct method, noncash items such as depreciation, amortization, and the like are ignored and therefore omitted from the statement of cash flows.

24. Regardless of which method is used, the formal statement of cash flows is always divided into three parts: cash flows from operating activities, cash flows from investing activities, and cash flows from financing activities.

Using Information From the Statement of Cash Flows to Make Decisions

25. By highlighting cash inflows and outflows during a period, the statement of cash flows helps investors and creditors assess the timing, amounts, and uncertainty of future cash flows. It helps users compare the financial policies of different firms and answers such questions as whether or not a company is expanding or retrenching; increasing or decreasing its reliance on operating income, debt, or equity financing; and how new buildings, other investments, and even dividends are being paid for.

26. We can learn a great deal about a company by analyzing patterns that appear among the three cash flow categories in a statement of cash flows.

COMMON ERRORS

The three most difficult aspects of this chapter, and hence the reasons for the most common student errors, are:

1. Properly classifying cash flows as operating, investing, or financing activities.

2. Adjusting reported net income to cash flow provided by (used in) operations when using the indirect method.

3. Converting revenues and expenses to cash inflows and outflows when using the direct method.

1. Properly Classifying Cash Flows as Operating, Investing, or Financing Activities

Exhibit 4 in chapter 14 of the text will help you learn the proper classification of cash flows. Basically, any cash inflows from activities whose revenue would be reported on the income statement are operating activities. Included in this category are interest revenue and dividend revenue, which students may be tempted to classify as financing activities. Cash outflows are the expenses reported on the income statement, except for depreciation and similar noncash expenses.

Included in investing activities are purchases and sales of all noncurrent assets and investments other than trading securities and the making or collecting of loans. Sometimes students are tempted to include cash flows from the nontrading securities transactions in operating activities, but they should be classified as investing activities.

Finally, financing activities include all borrowing and repayments, the issuance or purchase of stock, and the payments of dividends. Be careful to include the proceeds of short-term as well as long-term debt as a financing activity.

2. Adjusting Reported Net Income to Cash Flow Provided by (Used in) Operations When Using the Indirect Method

The best way to understand how to adjust net income to cash flow provided by (used in) operations is to consider the following.

a. Decreases in accounts receivable are added to net income because some of the receivable balance from last period has been collected during the current period. Therefore, cash collected is greater than reported revenue. Similarly, decreases in other current assets are added because some of the assets purchased last period have been used this period. Therefore, the reported expenses are greater than cash paid for expenses.

b. Increases in accounts receivable are subtracted from net income because some of this period's sales are not yet collected. Similarly, increases in other current assets are subtracted because cash has been spent to buy assets that have not yet been used in operations and therefore have not yet been recognized as expenses.

c. Increases in current operating payables are added to net income because the liability for expense has not yet been paid. Therefore, the reported expense exceeds cash paid. Conversely, decreases in current operating payables mean more cash was spent than had been reported as an expense, and so net income must be reduced to determine cash inflow from operations.

d. All noncash items such as depreciation and amortization must be added back to net income because they were expenses that did not require any cash.

e. The adjustments needed can be summarized as follows:

Net income	xxxx
+ Noncash expenses (e.g., depreciation).......................	xx
− Increases in current operating assets...........................	(xx)
+ Decreases in current operating assets...........................	xx
+ Increases in current operating payables......................	xx
− Decreases in current operating payables......................	(xx)
= Net cash flow provided by (used in) operating activities......................	xxxx

3. **Converting Revenues and Expenses to Cash Inflows and Outflows When Using the Direct Method**

Be sure to understand the logic of converting from accrual to cash amounts before relying on the guidelines given in the chapter. For example, in trying to understand how sales revenue is converted to cash receipts from customers, use logic such as sales for the period plus beginning receivables is all that could have been collected. And if there were no receivables at the end of the period, then all the cash would have been collected during the period. However, the amount of receivables at the end of the period must be subtracted (because it wasn't collected), so sales plus beginning receivables minus ending receivables equals cash receipts from customers. Similar logic can be used for expenses. For example, reported interest expense plus the beginning balance in Interest Payable is the total amount of interest that could have been paid during the period. And if there were no ending Interest Payable, all the cash would have been paid. If there is an ending balance in Interest Payable, interest expense plus the beginning payable balance minus the ending payable balance equals cash payments for interest. All other revenues and expenses would be similarly converted, except insurance expense, which is usually purchased (and is an asset) before it is an expense, and cost of goods sold, which must be converted to purchases and then to cash paid for inventory purchased.

SELF-TEST

Matching

Instructions: Write the letter of each of the following terms in the space to the left of its appropriate definition.

a. cash equivalents   e. direct method
b. operating activities   f. indirect method
c. statement of cash flows   g. financing activities
d. cash flows

_____   1. The financial resources that flow into and out of a company.

_____   2. A method of reporting the net cash flow from operations that converts accrual net income to a cash basis.

_____   3. Transactions and events whereby resources are obtained from or repaid to owners and creditors.

_____   4. The primary financial report that shows the inflows and outflows of cash for a given period.

_____   5. Transactions and events that are used in the determination of net income.

_____   6. Highly liquid investments that are easily converted to cash.

_____   7. A method of reporting the net cash flow from operations that shows the main classes of cash receipts and cash payments.

True/False

Instructions: Place a check mark in the appropriate column to indicate whether each of the following statements is true or false.

	True	False
1. The statement of cash flows is a primary financial statement, along with the income statement and the balance sheet.	_____	_____
2. The statement of cash flows is the connecting link between two income statements.	_____	_____
3. The statement of cash flows is usually prepared for the same time period covered by the corresponding income statement.	_____	_____
4. Dividend receipts would be included in the amount of cash provided by operating activities.	_____	_____
5. The primary purpose of the statement of cash flows is to provide information about the profitability of an entity for a given period of time.	_____	_____
6. Cash generated by operations is equal to the net income for the period less dividends paid or declared.	_____	_____
7. When the direct method is used to prepare a statement of cash flows, depreciation is added back to net income.	_____	_____
8. The issuance of stock for the purchase of land is reported as a financing activity on the statement of cash flows.	_____	_____
9. The indirect method of preparing a statement of cash flows involves adding back noncash expenses to net income in arriving at net cash flow provided by (used in) operations.	_____	_____
10. An increase in the Accounts Payable balance over the year is added to net income when the statement of cash flows is prepared using the direct method.	_____	_____
11. The statement of cash flows provides investors with information that helps users assess the amounts, timing, and uncertainty of future cash flows.	_____	_____
12. The statement of cash flows is not covered by the auditor's opinion.	_____	_____
13. Cash generated by operations will be the same under both the indirect and the direct methods of preparing a statement of cash flows.	_____	_____

	True	False

14. A decrease in the Inventory balance for the period is added to net income in computing cash generated from operations with the indirect method. .... _____ _____

15. A decrease in the Accounts Receivable balance is subtracted from net income in computing cash generated from operations by the indirect method. .... _____ _____

16. Since the statement of cash flows uses the same information found in comparative balance sheets and income statements, it is always the least useful of the three primary financial statements. .... _____ _____

Multiple Choice

Instructions: Circle the letter that best completes each of the following statements.

1. Which of the following is *least* likely to be classified as a cash equivalent?

   a. Commercial paper
   b. Investments in short-term bonds
   c. U.S. Treasury bills
   d. Certificates of deposit

2. Which of the following would *not* be reported on a statement of cash flows prepared using the indirect method?

   a. The amortization of patents
   b. Fully depreciated machinery that was scrapped during the year
   c. Treasury stock that has been purchased from a stockholder
   d. Depreciation expense for the year

3. Which of the following groups of business activities is *not* a required classification on the statement of cash flows?

   a. Operating activities
   b. Financing activities
   c. Cash activities
   d. Investing activities

4. When the indirect method is used to prepare a statement of cash flows, depreciation is treated as an adjustment to reported net income because it

   a. is a source of cash.
   b. reduces reported net income but does not involve an outflow of cash.
   c. reduces reported net income and involves an inflow of cash.
   d. is an inflow of cash to a reserve account for the replacement of assets.

5. Which of the following would be reported on a statement of cash flows prepared using the direct method?

   a. Total wages paid during the year
   b. Depreciation expense for the year
   c. Accrual-basis net income
   d. An increase in the Accounts Receivable balance for the year

6. Which of the following is considered an operating activity?

   a. The purchase of a building
   b. The payment of dividends to stockholders
   c. The repayment of the principal on a loan
   d. The payment of interest to creditors

7. The direct method of preparing a statement of cash flows

   a. is usually the easiest method to implement.
   b. is usually more straightforward than the indirect method and thus may be easier to understand.
   c. generally produces a higher net cash flow figure than the indirect method.
   d. involves a reconciliation between net income and net cash flows from operating activities.

Use the following information to answer Questions 8–10.
Following are the Machinery and Accumulated Depreciation—Machinery accounts as they looked after transactions for the year had been reported. (Note that some entries were intentionally omitted.)

Machinery

Beg. Bal.	120,000	Sale of Machinery	40,000
End. Bal.	160,000		

Accumulated Depreciation—Machinery

Sale of Machinery	26,000	Beg. Bal.	38,000
		End. Bal.	64,000

8. The cost of machinery acquired during the period (assuming cash purchases) was

   a. $38,000.
   b. $64,000.
   c. $120,000.
   d. $80,000.

9. The book value of machinery sold during the period was

   a. $14,000.
   b. $28,000.
   c. $38,000.
   d. $40,000.

10. The depreciation expense that would be added back to net income in computing cash from operations under the indirect method was

    a. $26,000.
    b. $38,000.
    c. $40,000.
    d. $52,000.

11. Which of the following transactions would *not* appear on a statement of cash flows prepared by the direct method?

    a. A net loss from operations
    b. The amount paid to acquire treasury stock
    c. Payment of last year's federal income tax liability
    d. The payment of cash dividends that were declared last year

12. Baker Company issued stock to Taylor Company in exchange for equipment. This transaction would be reflected in

    a. a narrative explanation or in a separate schedule.
    b. the operating activities section of a statement of cash flows.
    c. the financing activities section of a statement of cash flows.
    d. the investing activities section of a statement of cash flows.

13. The statement of cash flows discloses changes in the cash and cash-equivalent accounts during the year and
    a. summarizes the operating, financing, and investing activities of an entity.
    b. includes transactions that affect an entity's prior financial position.
    c. reports significant changes in net income.
    d. measures the overall profitability of an entity.

14. Clark Company had the following operating results for 2006:

Beginning Inventory	$ 200,000
Ending Inventory	180,000
Cost of Goods Sold	1,150,000
Beginning Accounts Payable	45,000
Ending Accounts Payable	65,000

    How much cash did Clark pay for inventory in 2006?
    a. $1,170,000
    b. $1,110,000
    c. $1,150,000
    d. $1,190,000

Use the following financial information to answer Questions 15–17.

	2006	2005
Cash	$ 35,000	$ 20,000
Other current assets	175,000	130,000
Equipment	400,000	320,000
Accumulated depreciation	(140,000)	(120,000)
Land	40,000	36,000
Current liabilities	60,000	40,000
Bonds payable	100,000	50,000
Common stock	300,000	270,000
Retained earnings	50,000	26,000

Additional information:
- No equipment was sold during the year.
- Dividends for the year 2006 were $12,000.
- Retained Earnings was affected only by net income and dividends.
- All changes in the current accounts were from operating activities.

15. Cash provided by operating activities amounted to
    a. $11,000.
    b. $76,000.
    c. $31,000.
    d. $56,000.

16. Cash provided by (used in) investing activities amounted to
    a. $84,000.
    b. $(84,000).
    c. $80,000.
    d. $(80,000).

17. Cash provided by financing activities amounted to:
    a. $80,000.
    b. $38,000.
    c. $18,000.
    d. $68,000.

Exercises

E14-1   Statement of Cash Flows Classifications

Sound Company had the following transactions during 2006.

Cash sales totaled $750,000.
Purchased land and building for $200,000.
Paid $25,000 of cash dividends that were declared in 2005.
Issued long-term bonds of $250,000.
Paid interest on long-term bonds of $25,000.
Purchased inventory for $75,000 cash.
Received $50,000 worth of inventory in exchange for common stock.
Paid taxes of $32,000 for the year.
Purchased treasury stock for $15,000.

Instructions: Based on the above transactions, compute the amount of cash provided by operating, investing, and financing activities for 2006.

E14-2   Converting Accrual Amounts to Cash Basis

The 2006 and 2005 balance sheets and additional information for Suarez Company are presented below.

Suarez Company
Balance Sheets
As of December 31, 2006 and 2005

Assets	2006	2005
Cash and cash equivalents	$ 8,000	$ 5,000
Accounts receivable	65,000	45,000
Interest receivable	1,500	2,000
Inventory	50,000	40,000
Equipment	150,000	100,000
Accumulated depreciation	(60,000)	(40,000)
Total assets	$214,500	$152,000
Liabilities and Stockholders' Equity		
Accounts payable	$ 32,000	$ 18,000
Wages payable	24,000	12,000
Capital stock	100,000	100,000
Retained earnings	58,500	22,000
Total liabilities and stockholders' equity	$214,500	$152,000

Additional information:
   a. 2006 sales totaled $521,500.
   b. Interest revenue was $20,000.
   c. Cost of goods sold was $350,000.
   d. Wages expense was $125,000.
   e. No equipment was retired during the year.
   f. Dividends of $10,000 were paid in December 2006.

Instructions: Compute the following for 2006.

   1. Cash collected from customers.

   2. Cash received from interest revenue.

   3. Cash paid for inventory.

4. Cash wages paid to employees.

E14-3   Cash Flows from Operations (Direct Method)

Partial 2006 and 2005 financial statements for White Company are presented below.

White Company
Partial Balance Sheets
December 31, 2006 and 2005

	2006	2005
Current Assets		
Cash	$ 40,000	$ 30,000
Accounts receivable	70,000	66,000
Inventory	60,000	66,000
Prepaid insurance	4,000	3,000
Total current assets	$174,000	$165,000
Current Liabilities		
Accounts payable	$150,000	$145,000
Notes payable	25,000	0
Wages payable	12,000	14,000
Total current liabilities	$187,000	$159,000

White Company
Partial Income Statement
For the Year Ending December 31, 2006

Sales revenue		$150,000
Cost of goods sold:		
Beginning inventory	$ 66,000	
Purchases	80,000	
Cost of goods available for sale	$146,000	
Ending inventory	60,000	
Cost of goods sold		86,000
Gross margin		$ 64,000
Wages expense	$ 50,000	
Insurance expense	9,000	
Depreciation expense	10,000	69,000
Net income (loss)		$ (5,000)

Instructions: 1. Compute the cash received from sales.

2. Compute the cash paid for inventory, insurance, and wages.

3. Using the direct method, compute the total cash inflow (outflow) from operating activities.

E14-4   Cash Flows from Operations (Indirect Method)

Use the information for White Company in E14-3 to compute by the indirect method the net cash inflow (outflow) from operating activities.

E14-5   Cash Flow Provided by (Used in) Operating Activities (Indirect Method)

Income statement data for Crane Corporation for the year are as follows.

Net income before depreciation	$ 60,000
Depreciation expense	(22,000)
	$ 38,000
Gain on sale of long-term investments	3,000
	$ 41,000
Loss on sale of equipment	(8,000)
Income before taxes	$ 33,000
Income taxes	(12,000)
Net income	$ 21,000

Instructions: Prepare the cash flow provided by (used in) operating activities section of the statement of cash flows using the indirect method.

E14-6   Cash Flow Provided by (Used in) Operating Activities (Direct Method)

Michelle Oxborrow is the proprietor of a small bakery. The results of last year's operations and selected balance sheet data are shown below.

Sales revenue	$300,000	
Cost of goods sold	170,000	
Gross margin		$130,000
Operating expenses:		
Salaries expense	$ 55,000	
Insurance expense	5,000	
Rent expense	17,000	
Utilities expense	3,000	80,000
Net income		$ 50,000

	Beginning of Year	End of Year
Accounts receivable	$ 15,000	$ 23,000
Inventory	20,000	17,500
Prepaid insurance	5,000	3,500
Accounts payable	10,000	20,000
Salaries payable	8,000	6,000

Instructions: From the information provided, determine the amount of net cash flow provided from operations, using the direct method. (Use the form on the following page for your answer.)

E14-7   Cash Flow Provided by (Used in) Operating Activities (Indirect Method)

Given the data in E14-6, show how the amount of net cash flow from operating activities would be calculated using the indirect method.

E14-6 (concluded)

ANSWERS

Matching

1.	d	4.	c	6.	a
2.	f	5.	b	7.	e
3.	g				

True/False

1.	T	7.	F	12.	F
2.	F	8.	F	13.	T
3.	T	9.	T	14.	T
4.	T	10.	F	15.	F
5.	F	11.	T	16.	F
6.	F				

Multiple Choice

1.	b	7.	b	13.	a
2.	b	8.	d	14.	b
3.	c	9.	a	15.	c
4.	b	10.	d	16.	b
5.	a	11.	a	17.	d
6.	d	12.	a		

Exercises

E14-1   Statement of Cash Flows Classifications

Cash Flow from Operating Activities
Receipts:
Sales.. $ 750,000

Payments:
Inventory...	$(75,000)	
Interest	(25,000)	
Taxes..	(32,000)	(132,000)
Total		$ 618,000

Cash Flow from Investing Activities
Payments:
Land and building.. $(200,000)

Cash Flow from Financing Activities
Receipts:
Long-term bonds... $ 250,000

Payments:
Dividends..	$(25,000)	
Treasury stock..	(15,000)	(40,000)
Total..		$ 210,000

E14-2   Converting Accrual Amounts to Cash Basis

1. Cash collected from customers:

2006 Sales	$521,500
Beginning accounts receivable	45,000
Ending accounts receivable	(65,000)
Cash collected from sales	$501,500

2. Cash received from interest revenue:

Interest revenue	$ 20,000
Beginning interest receivable	2,000
Ending interest receivable	(1,500)
Cash collected from interest	$ 20,500

3. Cash paid for inventory:

Cost of goods sold	$350,000
Ending inventory	50,000
Beginning inventory	(40,000)
Purchases	$360,000
Beginning accounts payable	18,000
Ending accounts payable	(32,000)
Cash paid for inventory	$346,000

4. Cash wages paid to employees:

Wages expense	$125,000
Beginning wages payable	12,000
Ending wages payable	(24,000)
Cash paid for wages	$113,000

E14-3   Cash Flows from Operations (Direct Method)

1.

Sales revenue	$150,000
+ Beginning accounts receivable balance	66,000
− Ending accounts receivable balance	(70,000)
Cash received from sales	$146,000

2.

Cost of goods sold	$ 86,000
+ Ending inventory balance	60,000
− Beginning inventory balance	(66,000)
= Purchases	$ 80,000
+ Beginning accounts payable balance	145,000
− Ending accounts payable balance	(150,000)
Cash payments for inventory	$ 75,000

Insurance expense	$ 9,000
+ Ending prepaid insurance balance	4,000
− Beginning prepaid insurance balance	(3,000)
Cash payments for insurance	$ 10,000

Wages expense	$ 50,000
+ Beginning wages payable balance	14,000
− Ending wages payable balance	(12,000)
Cash paid for wages	$ 52,000

3.   **White Company**
                          Cash Flow from Operating Activities

Cash receipts from sales		$146,000
Cash payments for:		
Inventory	$75,000	
Insurance	10,000	
Wages...	52,000	137,000
Net cash flow provided by operating activities		$ 9,000

E14-4   Cash Flows from Operations (Indirect Method)

                                    White Company
                          Cash Flow from Operating Activities

Net income (loss)		$(5,000)
Add (deduct) adjustments to cash basis:		
Depreciation expense	$10,000	
Increase in accounts receivable	(4,000)	
Decrease in inventory..	6,000	
Increase in prepaid insurance	(1,000)	
Increase in accounts payable	5,000	
Decrease in wages payable.....................................	(2,000)	14,000
Net cash flow provided by operating activities		$ 9,000

The following worksheet is useful in solving E14-3 and E14-4.

	Income Statement	Adjustments	Cash Flows	
Sales	150,000	−4,000	146,000	Adjustment for A/R
Cost of Goods Sold	−86,000	6,000	−75,000	Adjustment for Inventory
		5,000		Adjustment for A/P
Wages Expense	−50,000	−2,000	−52,000	Adjustment for Wages Payable
Insurance Expense	−9,000	−1,000	−10,000	Adjustment for Prepaid Insurance
Depreciation Expense	−10,000	10,000	0	Adjustment for noncash item
Net Income	−5,000		9,000	Cash from operations

E14-5   Cash Flow Provided by (Used in) Operating Activities (Indirect Method)

Net income...		$21,000
Add: Depreciation expense	$22,000	
Loss on sale of equipment......................................	8,000	30,000
Subtract: Gain on sale of long-term investments		(3,000)
Net cash flow provided by operating activities.............		$48,000

E14-6   Cash Flow Provided by (Used in) Operating Activities (Direct Method)

Sales Revenue	$300,000	
+ Beginning accounts receivable	15,000	
– Ending accounts receivable	(23,000)	
Total cash receipts		$292,000
Cost of goods sold	$170,000	
+ Ending inventory	17,500	
– Beginning inventory	(20,000)	
Purchases	$167,500	
+ Beginning accounts payable	10,000	
– Ending accounts payable	(20,000)	
Cash paid to suppliers for inventory	$157,500	
Salaries expense	$ 55,000	
+ Beginning salaries payable	8,000	
– Ending salaries payable	(6,000)	
Cash paid to employees	$ 57,000	
Utilities expense (no adjustment required)	$ 3,000	
Rent expense (no adjustment required)	$ 17,000	
Insurance expense	$ 5,000	
+ Ending prepaid insurance	3,500	
– Beginning prepaid insurance	(5,000)	
Cash paid for insurance	$ 3,500	
Total cash payments		238,000
Net cash flow provided from operations		$ 54,000

E14-7   Cash Flow Provided by (Used in) Operating Activities (Indirect Method)

Net income	$ 50,000
Add (deduct) adjustments to cash basis:	
Increase in accounts receivable	(8,000)
Decrease in inventory	2,500
Decrease in prepaid insurance	1,500
Increase in accounts payable	10,000
Decrease in salaries payable	(2,000)
Net cash flow provided from operations	$ 54,000

The following worksheet is helpful in explaining the adjustments required for E14-6 and E14-7.

	Income Statement	Adjustments	Cash Flows	
Sales	300,000	–8,000	292,000	Adjustment for A/R
Cost of Goods Sold	–170,000	2,500	–157,500	Adjustment for Inventory
		10,000		Adjustment for A/P
Salaries Expense	–55,000	–2,000	–57,000	Adjustment for Salaries Payable
Insurance Expense	–5,000	1,500	–3,500	Adjustment for Prepaid Insurance
Rent Expense	–17,000	0	–17,000	No adjustment
Utilities Expense	–3,000	0	–3,000	No adjustment
Net Income	50,000		54,000	Cash from operations